Ancient Scotland

KU-592-206

The standing stone of Clach na Tiompan, originally one of a set of four such monoliths, stands in a remote Highland setting beside the River Almond.

ANCIENT SCOTLAND

Stewart Ross

© Stewart Ross, 1991

First published 1991 by Lochar Publishing Ltd
This paperback edition published 1998 by
House of Lochar

All rights reserved. No part of this publication may be
reproduced, stored in a retrieval system, or transmitted,
in any form or by any means, electronic, mechanical,
photocopying, recording or otherwise, without the
prior permission of the publisher.

ISBN 1 899863 44 3

British Library Cataloguing in Publication Data
Ross, Stewart
　　Ancient Scotland.
　　1. Scotland, ancient period
　　I. Title
　　936.11

Printed in Hong Kong
for House of Lochar,
Isle of Colonsay, Argyll PA61 7YR, Scotland

FOR JAMES
who endured so many strange sites
with a patience belying his years

Contents

Acknowledgments

Every work of this nature is a corporate undertaking. While accepting full responsibility for all errors of fact and judgment, the author would like to thank a number of people for the immense help they have given him in preparing it: Anne Coppins for labouring day and night on the photographs, Julie Beer for producing fine drawings at very short notice, David Langworth for translating scribble into accurate and attractive maps, Graeme Stewart-Ross and Peter Henderson for kindly taking the trouble to read through the manuscript, Marjorie Henderson for her inimitable companionship on tours of ancient sites, Frances Kelly, literary agent, for setting up the project, James, Kate, Alexander and Eleanor for accepting that Auld Reekie was a no-go area for weeks, and Lucy for her proof reading, tolerance and constant encouragement.

All photographs were taken by the author, who is also responsible for the free translations of ancient texts which appear in the book.
   Drawings by Julie Beer.
   Maps by David Langworth.

Introduction

I am talking about barbarians. Tacitus

THIS BOOK is an attempt to breathe life into inanimate objects. While travelling through Scotland's rich and varied countryside, no tourist or native of that land can fail to notice the multitude of ancient monuments which lie on every hand. Some are little more than anonymous piles of stones, others are majestic and awe-inspiring remains of cultures long vanished. All are mysterious and difficult to interpret. A visit to a more recently occupied site, such as Stirling Castle, is instantly appealing: in the halls, battlements and statues we can recognise at once the aspirations of people not very different from ourselves. But what are we to make of a prehistoric ruin such as Cairnholy II, that strange empty tomb set on a lonely hillside above the waters of Wigtown Bay? Or of the shattered remnants of the Pictish fort at Dundurn, which once guarded the vital route along Strathearn from the neighbouring kingdom of Dalriada? After paying due recognition to their obvious aesthetic attraction, it is all too easy to dismiss them as bewilderingly obscure links with a remote and often unlettered past, whose anonymous heroes and incomprehensible customs appear irrelevant to the modern world.

Yet the past has no self-imposed boundaries. Prehistory slides into history just as the medieval period merges imperceptibly with the modern. The story of Scotland did not begin in the middle of the ninth century, when Kenneth mac Alpin was proclaimed king of both Picts and Scots. The first monarch of Alba and the society in which he lived were as much products of the past as were Keir Hardie and the early Labour Party. Fully to understand Scotland and her people, therefore, we need to look far back, to the time after the last ice age when human beings first drifted north into the Southern Uplands and beyond. For thousands of years the scene is cloudy and unfocused – not until the third century AD, for example, can we find a single Scotsman referred to by name – and we have to rely on the work of archaeologists rather than historians. But gradually the picture clears to the point where we can make out individual figures and reconstruct their lives with some accuracy.

There are several fine works on prehistoric Scotland, and many which take up the nation's history from Roman times or at the end of the Dark Ages. The pages which follow seek to bridge the gap between the two, tracing the development of the people of northern Britain from the earliest times to the point where the story becomes generally familiar and the visible remains readily identifiable. It is not necessarily an outline of progress. Indeed, it might be argued that in some spheres the people of ninth-century Scotland were impoverished compared with their distant ancestors. Be that as it may; if by the final line the reader feels a little more familiar with the ancient landscape, and not quite so ready to dismiss those who created it simply as barbarians (as Tacitus was prepared to do), then the purpose of this volume will have been achieved.

1

THE ARRIVAL
OF MAN

The Palaeolithic Age

MAN CAME late to Scotland. Although humanoid figures may have appeared on earth some four million years ago, it was another three million years before *Homo erectus* could be seen loping about the planet, and not until about 40,000 BC did the familiar *Homo sapiens sapiens* (Modern Man) replace Neanderthal Man as the predominant human species in Europe. As far as we know, the new creature stayed well away from the territory we now call Scotland for at least a further 32,000 years.

The reason for Modern Man's reluctance to migrate north was climatic. Over the last million years or so the earth has been subject to massive fluctuations in surface temperature, beside which current forecasts of global warming by a degree or two appear relatively unimportant. On at least four occasions the planet was gripped by prolonged *ice ages*, each lasting tens of thousands of years. These were interspersed by corresponding warm periods, known as interglacials, when the ice retreated and dense vegetation spread towards the poles. The pattern is complicated by the fact that neither the ice ages nor the more temperate periods between them were uniform in their arrival or withdrawal – there were brief warmings within the cold spells and cool periods during the interglacials. When the earth was at its hottest it is estimated that the sea rose some 35 metres above its present level, owing to the release of water from the polar ice caps. Broad deciduous forests of oak, elm and lime covered much of the lowland, where elephant, deer, wild oxen and boar abounded. In southern England our hirsute ancestors dwelt beside warm muddy rivers in which hippopotamuses lazed. If primitive Man did venture as far north as Scotland at this time, we have no record of his having done so.

The dense ice sheet rasped furthest south during the second or Anglian glaciation, when it reached the Thames Valley. It scoured the landscape so thoroughly that it is now well nigh impossible to work out in detail the appearance of the countryside before its advance. As the oceans around the poles froze, sea levels fell dramatically – as late as about 7000 BC, at about the time *Homo sapiens sapiens* was making his way into Scotland, a broad land-bridge extended between Britain and the Continent. Its northern shore ran from Lincolnshire to the tip of the Danish peninsular while, in the south, dry land stretched from East Sussex to part of the French coast south-west of where Le Touquet lies today. South of the ice sheet the landscape was reduced to a tundra-like barrenness, where woolly rhinoceros and mammoth, reindeer, bison and horses roamed in search of food. These conditions drove mammal life from northern Britain and all but obliterated traces of its existence there.

The glaciers of the last ice age, known technically as the Devonian glaciation, began to melt in about 15,000 BC, marking the end of what is known to archaeologists as the Palaeolithic period. Changes in climate occurred very slowly and erratically, so that Man was almost certainly unaware of their happening. But metre by metre, valley by valley, the ice cap retreated northwards, from its furthest extent in Yorkshire, to the Borders, the Highlands, over the northern isles and thence into the ocean beyond. The consequent rise in sea levels was to some extent compensated by a similar rise in the land, as if it were stretching itself now that it had been released from the dead weight it had borne for thousands of years. Thus in about 10,000 BC, like a great creature shedding a chrysalis of ice, the land we know as Scotland struggled into the sunlight.

Hunter-gatherers

Tundra gradually gave way to woodland, as first birch and pine then hazel trees seeded themselves in the fertile soil. By 5000 BC, as the world experienced one of its hotter spells, hardwood forests spread over wide expanses of the northern landscape. At this time, too, Scotland was becoming accustomed to another new arrival – Man. Students of prehistory (history before the advent of writing) used to lump together all civilisation before the Bronze Age as Stone Age. This has been shown to be a grossly oversimplified label, and we now divide the years between about 1,000,000 and 2000 BC into three periods: the Palaeolithic, Mesolithic and Neolithic, each of which in turn sub-divide into two or three sections. The first Scots (if we can take the liberty of calling them such) appear towards the close of the early Mesolithic period.

We can only surmise why small groups of primitive Stone Age people moved north into Scotland. The most likely explanation is that the steady rise in the level of the oceans, which made Britain an island in about 5500 BC, gradually drove westwards those living on the north-west facing coastal plain, now submerged beneath the North Sea. Turning north towards the higher land with relatively stable shorelines, they found the sort of environment which they favoured. With mean temperatures increasing century by century until about 3500 BC, the teeming virgin territory of Scotland was well able to provide them all that they required for survival. The warming of the climate has been put forward as another possible explanation for the migration. Afforestation led to animals which flourished in wide open spaces, such as mammoth, reindeer and bison, being replaced by woodland species, such as red deer and wild boar. Protected by the density of their natural habitat, these animals were less easily trapped or speared. It has been argued that the resulting food shortage led Man to move north in search of fresh hunting grounds. Given the tiny numbers of people involved, however, it is difficult to see why even in a wooded land there was not ample food for everyone. The fact is that we shall probably never know precisely why people first migrated into Scotland.

Accurate carbon dating, which can ascertain the age of carboniferous material up to 30,000 years old, enables us to establish a much tighter chronology for the Mesolithic period than for any of the preceding eras. Nevertheless, our knowledge of Britain's inhabitants living five or six thousand years before the birth of Christ remains very scant – our ignorance is certainly much greater than our knowledge. What is quite clear is that the peoples of north-western Europe were on the very fringes of civilisation. In 6000 BC the cultural and technological differences between the inhabitants of Scotland and the tribes of North Africa and the Near East were almost as striking as those between Europeans and Africans at the time of the Renaissance. While in Anatolia and the basin of the Euphrates city-dwelling Man was experimenting with woollen textiles, metalworking, pottery and the irrigation of farmland, his northern relatives were primitive hunter-gatherers. Arriving at a figure for the number of people living in Scotland at this time is largely guesswork. The population of the whole of Britain has been estimated at about 30,000, divided into what were probably family groups of between two and eight persons, though there is evidence indicating

Map 1
PREHISTORIC SCOTLAND

 Settlement

 Cairns and Tombs

 Stones and Circles

Iron Age Fort

Brochs

Orkney Isles

Knap of Howar • Papa Westray
Westray
Midhowe
Gurness
Skara Brae
Maes Howe
Kennibister
Ring of Brodgar
Unstan
Stenness Stones
Pentland Firth
Liddle • Isbister

Shetland Isles

Stanydale
Clickhimin
• Mousa
Jarlshof

Western Isles
Callanish
Harris
Northton
North Uist
South Uist
Dun Beag
Skye
Rhum
Dun Telve • Dun Troddan
Glenelg
Oronsay
Jura
Bute
Machrie Moor
Firth of Clyde

Dun Dornaigil
Dun Lagaidh
Achavanich • Camster
Hill o' Many Staines
North West Highlands
Moray Firth
Clava
Spey
Loanhead of Daviot
Cullerie
Dee
Balbridie
Grampian Mountains
The Caterthuns
Finavon
Carlungie
Broughty Ferry • Ardestie
Tay
Friarton Morton
Strontoiller
Kilmartin Valley
Forth
The Chesters
Traprain Law
Cairnpapple Hill
Pentland Hills • Castlelaw
Clyde
Edinshall
Firth of Forth
Cademuir
Dreva Craig
Tweed
Eildon Hills
• Hownam Rings
Southern Uplands
Twelve Apostles
Tyne
Torhousekie
Cairnholy I & II
Drumtroddan • Rispain Camp
Solway Firth

Nether Largie North Kilmartin
Mid Temple Wood
Nether Largie South
Ri Cruin
Achnabreck

0 _____ 40 m

that communities in the south may have contained as many as 25 people. Only a tiny fraction of the total lived above the Tees-Solway line, perhaps a maximum of about two dozen bands at any one time, giving Scotland a total population of no more than 150 souls. A figure so tiny is almost as difficult for us to comprehend as the millennial time scales with which prehistory confronts us. Some of the earliest sites of human habitation show clear signs of being occupied, albeit not continuously, for very long periods of time. But it is likely that a single natural disaster, such as a series of severe winters, could have halved the population or even wiped it out entirely for a while.

The hunter-gatherers of the Mesolithic period were nomadic. Drawing on such scant evidence as is available, experts have opined that during winter months they established temporary bases in areas where there was plentiful fresh water close to the sea, before setting off inland in pursuit of the deer herds in the spring. They may have travelled as far as 100 miles in a season. The best-known site of early settlement to be excavated is at Morton on Tentsmuir, north of St Andrews. When the place was first inhabited, 8000 years ago, the sea was about nine metres higher than at present, so that at high tide the Morton outcrop became an island. The remains of similar though later settlements have been uncovered at over 100 places around the country, notably at Dundee and Broughty Ferry on Tayside, on the isles of Rum and Oronsay, at Campbeltown and Oban in Argyll, along the Dee and Ythan Rivers in Grampian, at Redpoint on Loch Torridon, and along the banks of the Forth and Clyde. As far as we can tell, those who rested for a while at these points put up no substantial or permanent buildings. At Cnoc Coig on Oronsay, archaeologists have come across what may be the post-holes of some form of windbreak or tent, but so far there has been no evidence to suggest substantial stone or timber dwellings. On their summer forays the hunters must have slept in the open, sheltered in caves or rested beneath light tents made from sticks and animal skins.

The First Settlements

A picture of how these people lived has to be produced from the scant evidence uncovered at the sites, such as Morton, where they remained long enough to leave permanent traces of their stay. These invariably take the form of rubbish found within the huge middens which are a striking feature of early settlements. It is crucial to bear in mind, of course, that this was a society which existed for about 2000 years – a period as long as the whole of the Christian era – during which there must have been changes in lifestyle. The evidence from a single settlement, therefore, has to be interpreted with caution, and cannot safely be employed, even tentatively, to produce a complete reconstruction of Mesolithic Scotland. However, there are a number of features of which we can be certain. We know, for example, that they had fire, because charcoal and pyrite have been found, the latter undoubtedly employed to make sparks. Fires kept away predators, provided warmth and enabled food to be cooked. It is likely that it was also employed in ritual. Since there is no evidence that these wandering people knew how to make pots, the only form of cooking would have been roasting.

The most important remains from the Mesolithic period are tools of one sort or another. The simplest and earliest ones are made from flint or, more commonly in Scotland, hard igneous and metamorphic rocks selected because they could be chipped away to form tough, sharp implements for hacking and scraping. It is not always easy to work out what a piece of roughly-shaped stone or bone was used for. Indeed, to the untrained eye, many so-called 'implements', especially the multi-purpose lumps of stone known as hand axes, are virtually indistinguishable from the sort of rocks one comes across every day on the beach or in a field. More recognisable are slivers of stone crudely fashioned into harpoon, spear or arrow heads. Later, more sophisticated bone and antler artefacts appear, sometimes in the shape of rudimentary mattocks. Whatever purpose

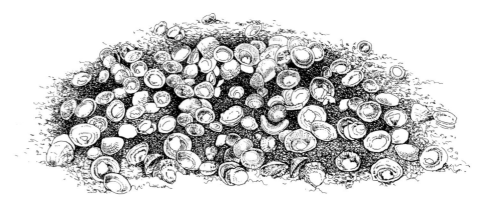

Gigantic shell-filled middens are almost the only visible remains of settlements used by Scotland's earliest inhabitants.

The coast near Benane Head, Strathclyde. Scotland's Mesolithic inhabitants gathered all kinds of shellfish from the shore to supplement their diet of meat, nuts and berries.

these served, however, it was not agriculture. Mesolithic Man was not a farmer.

The tangible remains of these early settlements suggest initially that their inhabitants survived on a diet consisting almost exclusively of meat and various *fruit de mer*. Because they required no hunting or netting, shell-clad creatures from the shoreline were an obvious choice. The immense heaps of discarded shells near places of habitation reveal that crabs, oysters and especially easily-gathered limpets were the most popular crustacean fare. At Caisteal nan Gillean on Oronsay, for example, there is a midden dating from about 5000 BC which is 30 metres in diameter and filled with millions of shells, mixed with bones, to a depth of three and a half metres. The island camp sites also reveal a wide variety of fish bones (including saithe, eel, haddock and bream) as well as the bones of seabirds such as cormorants, gulls and gannets. Animal bones are rare, though it does appear that seals were eaten. The presence of antlers may be explained by their usefulness as tools. On mainland sites the remains of cod, salmon and sturgeon have been uncovered, intermingled with the bones of larger beasts, particularly deer. In the muddy banks of the Forth even whale bones have been found: scavengers must have come across the creatures stranded on the shore and hacked them to pieces for food. How they set about butchering such enormous mammals with only stone and bone tools remains an intriguing mystery. Small fish were probably harpooned, trapped in pools or caught in nets made from thin leather thongs. Larger beasts were no doubt brought down from a distance by spears or arrows, then clubbed to death by stone axes. In such a society, physical prowess and dexterity were no doubt highly prized.

It is probably incorrect to make too many assumptions about the carnivorous habits of our distant ancestors. Though it is tempting to infer from the contents of their middens that they feasted largely off roasted meat, fish or fowl, it is more likely that they were at least as omnivorous as ourselves. For much of the time they had to consume whatever was to hand. It is reasonable to suggest that normally this was not meat, which required the effort and patience of hunting, but the edible fruits, berries and plants which could easily be plucked from the countryside. But organic matter soon breaks down, and the only vegetarian remains from the Mesolithic larder which survive are hazelnut shells. Winter must have been an abysmally cruel time for these scavenging people. Presumably one reason why they lived in comparatively small groups was that without agriculture or some system of food storage it was easier to survive the lean months in family units rather than in larger bands. The carcass of a single deer could have

A storm over Loch Cluanie. It is now difficult to imagine that in early prehistoric times, when the climate was warmer than it is today, dense forest covered much of the Highlands.

sustained four or five people for weeks, provided they knew how to preserve the flesh by salting or drying.

Almost nothing is known about how groups communicated between themselves or with outsiders. They must have had some form of language, though we do not know to what extent it differed between groups. Did hunters fight when they came across each other? Did they co-operate in the chase, or merely skulk cautiously past each other on opposite sides of the glade? Family units may well have viewed the territory around their winter base camp as somehow reserved to themselves, but this does not necessarily imply that they would have regarded visitors with hostility. Aboriginal people in other parts of the world, whose lifestyles have survived until comparatively recently, rarely display the same jealous possessiveness as modern Man, and there is nothing to suggest that men of the Middle Stone Age employed any form of fortification or instrument of war.

There is some evidence that towards the latter half of the Mesolithic period artefacts were being exchanged over quite long distances. We cannot tell, however, whether this was the result of elementary trade, or pillage. A canoe hewn from a log of Scots Pine has been discovered in the mud of Friarton, near Perth. Though this represents one of the most sophisticated technological developments of the age, we know neither the vessel's primary purpose (fishing

An artist's reconstruction of prehistoric canoes, based on the remains of such vessels uncovered in England. It was probably in boats like these that Man first crossed to the Western Isles.

or travel for trade), nor how numerous such conveyances were. The early pioneers who settled on some of the Hebridean islands (and Papa Westray from about 5000 BC) must have travelled thither by boat, implying that they could construct and pilot quite seaworthy vessels. But we do not know whether these were simply large dug-out canoes, or more elaborate coracles.

Human Touches

Three further examples of archaeological discovery offer still more tantalizing pieces of the fragmented jig-saw puzzle of life at this time. In England, at least, from about 7000 BC we can identify the practice of burying the dead. This almost certainly implies some form of religious life. It may be argued that simply to be human is to be religious; at any rate, given the precariousness of their existence, their terrifying ignorance of the nature of the world around them and the sophisticated religious practice of their immediate successors, it is inconceivable that early *Homo sapiens sapiens* did not spend at least some time trying to curry favour with the capricious powers which appeared to control their world.

The discoveries of what appear to be decorative beads and the bones of domesticated wolves, the forerunners of our dogs, lend further colour to an otherwise frustratingly grey picture. These finds suggest that the earliest inhabitants of Scotland welcomed animal companionship and had an appreciation of beauty, thus helping to soften an impression of unrelieved barbarism. Unfortunately we are still left with an incomplete mosaic. Even making every possible inference from our present knowledge, we cannot be sure what sort of people we are talking about. We do not know what they looked like, what they sounded like or even what they did for much of the time.

In the absence of hard evidence, those of an optimistic or romantic disposition are tempted to conjure up an image of Mesolithic Scotland peopled by a communistic noble savage, living uncorrupted by materialism in instinctive harmony with both nature and his fellow beings. The favoured image is of a tight family group squatting around a fire on a summer's evening, satiated with succulent limpets and fresh fruit, and gazing out over a clear, unpolluted sea. To those of a Hobbesian disposition this is an impossibly unrealistic pipe dream: they can conceive only of savages whose brutish and short lives were nothing but a struggle for survival, plagued by disease and every conceivable misanthropy. They would have us conceive of a bleak, snow-covered landscape, in which

The vast wilderness of Sutherland, little changed from the landscape which emerged at the end of the last ice age, some 17,000 years ago.

scrawny half-human creatures huddle around a wretched little tent-like structure and squabble over a few scraps of blackened and festering flesh.

Based upon extreme views of human nature rather than fact, neither of these interpretations is satisfactory. Since it is improbable that the fundamental personality of Man has changed much over the last few millennia, the men and women who first colonised Scotland were unlikely to have differed radically from ourselves. Certainly, they must have been tough, for only the fittest could have survived, and there was little room for sentimentality in their Spartan culture. Suffering, whether of Man or beast, was probably regarded with an equanimity which we would find distressing. But no doubt truth and beauty, cruelty and treachery played as great a part in their lives as they do in ours. They must have laughed and shed tears as we do, and when they gazed at the sun setting over the Western Isles they were no doubt filled with the same sense of wonder as twentieth-century observers. For all its vaunted technological achievement and conceited belief in self-defined progress, our civilisation is painfully brittle. Should it ever be overtaken by some sort of global catastrophe, within a century or so the handful of survivors might well find themselves scrabbling for limpets along the shoreline, just as their ancestors had done 7000 years before.

2

CIVILISATION

Agriculture

THE TRANSFORMATION of a nomadic society into one of permanent agricultural settlement is probably the most important single change made by Man since his appearance on the earth. For all practical purposes he became virtually a different animal. During the Neolithic period (c. 4500 BC to c. 2000 BC) he developed from a hunter-scavenger, a slave of the environment who lived in small groups and left virtually no record of his presence on the planet, into a creature capable of adapting the world around to suit his needs through unprecedented co-operation with his fellow human beings. For the first time we can recognise a distinct people.

Despite the tardy pace of change in the Neolithic world compared with that of our own day, Scotland's abundance of monuments and relics from this era testifies to the vibrancy of a culture that was clearly neither static nor monolithic. Nevertheless, information relating to the more mundane aspects of social life, such as farming, fishing and housing, is still sadly deficient. Snippets of evidence – like individual frames selected at random from a reel of film – are extremely difficult to place in the correct order, and rarely do we have fragments which can confidently be placed alongside each other in sequence. As a result, analysis of this crucial stage of human development is tentative and incomplete.

There are a number of theories about how farming spread to Britain from the western Mediterranean, where it was being practised by about 6500 BC. One view, now largely discarded, is that there was a full-scale westwards migration of people skilled in agriculture. The logistical difficulties of mounting this sort of prehistoric Great Trek are obvious, leading to the second suggestion that after small numbers of farmers had crossed the Channel with livestock and seedcorn, and established themselves close to the southern shores, their practices were soon adopted by the indigenous population (a process known as acculturation) and spread swiftly over the whole island. By following the shoreline it was perfectly feasible for native or Continental navigators to venture northwards, settling near sheltered coves or estuaries where the soil was light and easily worked. Some immigrants may have avoided the south-east altogether and put ashore further up the British coast. This would explain as adequately as the colonisation theory why agriculture seems to have been adopted in places as far apart as East Anglia and eastern Scotland at about the same time.

A third explanation for the way agriculture arrived in the British Isles suggests that, in the south at least, Mesolithic society was more adventurous than it has been given credit for: native fishermen or traders, learning about agriculture during their continental sojourns, returned with their newly-acquired knowledge, animals and grain to establish farms of their own at home. It may well be that the first British farming resulted from a combination of several forms of introduction – all we know for certain is that by about 4000 BC there were agricultural communities in Scotland.

The change from a hunter-gatherer to an agrilcultural way of life was probably less traumatic than might be imagined, for early in the fourth millennium BC the native inhabitants of Britain may already have been undertaking rudimentary management of deer herds, thereby facilitating their hunting and ensuring a more regular food supply. In some areas forest clearance had begun, too, a process which accelerated rapidly with the arrival of crop farming. Furthermore, the old ways did not die out completely. Families of hunter-gatherers survived in remoter districts, such as the island of Jura, until the middle of the third millennium BC, and bands of farmers also went on hunting and fishing expeditions to supplement local fare with the abundant fresh food found in the woods, rivers and seas.

It is not difficult to imagine why people were attracted to a more settled and secure existence. Agriculture promised to provide a more reliable food supply, and some of its produce could be stored fairly easily for use during the winter months. Moreover, when families lived in the same region for several generations they could afford to spend time constructing substantial, comfortable dwellings and undertake other projects requiring considerable manpower over long periods of time.

It is less easy to see what drew Continental immigrants to Britain, if that is indeed what happened. Since the post-glacial warming was past its peak by about 3500 BC, it may be that in southern Europe there was insufficient easily-workable land to maintain the rising population, resulting in a slow migration to the north. Fishermen and even those standing on the French Channel coast would have caught glimpses of Britain. After initial reconnaissance trips, they may well have decided to settle in the fertile and comparatively under-populated island. The climate was more balmy than it is today. In lowland Scotland, average temperatures were probably akin to those currently experienced in southern Britain, making the region ripe for colonisation. The dense forests which had blanketed the land during the hottest millennia had now given way to broad mixed woodlands of pine, oak, willow, alder and birch, though it is thought likely that much of the north of the country was already treeless by about 3000 BC. There is some evidence that wind speeds increased in Neolithic times, leading to the formation of undulating sand-dunes near the northern coasts.

The first requirement of an agricultural community was land clearance. This laborious undertaking was never ending, since soil rapidly became exhausted when it was cultivated continuously for several seasons. While one patch was being farmed, therefore, nearby woodland was cleared to prepare it for sowing when, after about five or six years, the yield on the original plot had fallen to an unacceptable level. Modern experiments show that small trees, up to about the thickness of telegraph poles, can be felled with stone axes. Larger boles have to be stripped of bark near the base and left to die. The process can be hastened by burning. This has the added advantages of clearing brushwood and leaving a layer of potash fertiliser, which enriches the soil until washed away by the rains. For many years newly cleared fields were littered with tree stumps, which rotted away in the course of time to leave a chequered pattern of grazing and arable land not dissimilar to that which we see today. We have no record of Neolithic wooden fencing, though this must have been used to enclose cattle and protect arable fields from larger predators. In the vicinity of Stanydale Hall on Shetland the remains of ancient stone field walling have been identified. Some land was worked by single, self-sufficient farmsteads, but it is not known whether larger groups held their land in common or farmed individually-owned plots. It is likely that the land around settlements such as Skara Brae was cultivated by the whole village working together, thereby employing their limited resources to best effect. Livestock, too, was almost certainly owned communally.

Once a field had been cleared, the soil was prepared for planting by scratching at the surface with crude implements of bone or wood, known as digging sticks. Later, elementary single-furrow ploughs (known as ards) were devised, an

The long ruined cairn at Clach na Tiompan (Fife and Tayside Region). Built in the second and third millennia BC, it contained four separate burial chambers.

example of which has been uncovered on Shetland. Flax, rye, wheat and barley were the most common crops, the latter preponderating in the north. Flax strands, presumed to have been used for clothing manufacture at the very end of the period, have been discovered at Jarlshof on Shetland. The remains of barley grains found at Isbister (Orkney) were mixed with large quantities of weeds, reminding us how poor the crop yields were on these early farms. Cattle were kept for their meat, milk and hides. Sheep provided similar resources, though their straggly fleeces (more akin to hair than wool) made them unsuitable for cloth manufacture. Hogs were rarer in the north than the south – there is no evidence of their being raised on Harris, for example. The remains of ponies have been discovered on Shetland.

The transformation of Scotland between the fifth and fourth millennia BC was as complete as it was remarkable. In the course of a thousand years or less, a comparatively brief period in prehistoric terms, a nomadic society had been changed into an agricultural one. Man had started to tame the landscape and make nature his servant. He was no longer merely one among many species struggling for existence, but quite clearly the master. Nothing illustrates this new spirit of confident domination more clearly than the fine stone dwellings and monuments with which he began to transform the landscape.

Farmsteads and Villages

Throughout Britain, the great majority of Neolithic people not living in caves must have constructed dwellings of timber, the most readily available and easily worked building material. Unfortunately, in all but exceptional circumstances, organic compounds rot away, leaving no trace of the structure into which they had been fashioned. This is where students of Scottish prehistory are particularly fortunate: stone, not wood, was the favoured construction material in the north of the country, and through a lucky combination of human and geographical accidents a unique collection of Neolithic dwellings remains for us to inspect. In the care of the state and open to public view, the finest examples provide us with an evocative insight into a civilisation flourishing some three thousand years before the birth of Christ.

Despite higher mean temperatures and the consequent raised sea levels, there is evidence that during the fourth millennium the Orkney archipelago comprised fewer and larger islands, and the Orcadian island of Papa Westray may have been linked by a narrow neck of land to neighbouring Westray. If this were the case then Scotland's oldest extant homesteads on the Knap of Howar originally stood well inland beside fertile farmland, instead of holding their present exposed position close to Papa Westray's rocky shoreline. There are two Neolithic houses at Knap of Howar, each built in about 3400 BC. They are not the original buildings on the site. Displaying the same disregard for the noxious presence of centuries of refuse which we encountered with their Mesolithic forebears, the settlers at Knap of Howar sunk their houses deep in an existing midden, so they look like underground burrows, or prehistoric air-raid shelters. Though extremely unhygienic, the dwellings' design ensured that they were durable and warm, affording excellent protection against the elements. Moreover, since they were no doubt continually filled with acrid peat smoke, they would also have been comparatively midge-free. The roofs were canopies of turf, thatch or hide, resting on wooden spars supported from below, and presumably weighed down with stones to prevent their being blown away in the gales.

As far as we can tell, one of the pair of adjacent oval houses served as the dwelling quarters, the other slightly smaller one as a multi-purpose storeroom and workshop. The former, ten metres long by five metres wide, was divided by stone partitions into three sections, tentatively identified as areas for sleeping, cooking and general purposes. The doorway in each building faces the sea. Of greater interest are the details of personal life which can still be seen: the stone benches, hearths and alcoves used for stowing equipment and personal possessions. One of the most fascinating discoveries at Knap of Howar was a large quern, a stone basin for grinding corn and shells. The latter were milled into a fine powder then added to potters' clay as a strengthening agent. The small community appears to have been wholly self-sufficient, making its own utensils, tools and clothes, and sustaining itself on fish and home-produced food. The existence was certainly squalid and hard. But comfort is relative: compared with the precarious life of the nomad, the farmstead at Knap of Howar was luxury itself.

There is no way of telling to what extent the tiny settlement on Papa Westray was in any way typical of the way most families lived in the Scotland of the fourth millennium BC. The earliest remains at Jarlshof on Shetland comprise several oval houses, built in about 2400 BC. Their design and construction are similar to those at Knap of Howar, their trefoil-shaped ground plan being made up of a number of cells leading from a roughly circular central area. At Balbridie in Grampian and at Townhead on the Isle of Bute, archaeologists have uncovered the remains of what appear to have been large Neolithic timber halls. The great horseshoe-shaped stone house at Stanydale, with its curving facade reminiscent of that at Cairnholy I tomb in Dumfries and Galloway, appears to have been at the centre of a quite sizeable village. Were these larger buildings for assembly, or communal living? Did they belong to a tribal chief of some description, or were they publicly owned? The answers to these and similar questions on the social structure of ancient Scotland may always elude us, but they are still worth pursuing for the light they can shed on Man's development as a social being.

There is one more Stone Age settlement to which we have not yet referred: Skara Brae, undoubtedly the finest prehistoric monument in Scotland. It tells us more about the time when it was inhabited than all other domestic sites put together. Were it situated in a more southerly and accessible position, this unique village would probably rival Stonehenge for popularity.

During the winter of 1850 a great storm swept the Orkney and Shetland islands, whipping up the seas and throwing great clouds of sand away from the shoreline. When the tempest finally subsided a number of ancient stone buildings were noticed protruding from the dunes on the Bay of Skaill in Orkney. Those who first examined the site were uncertain of the age of the strange structures which had appeared overnight like mushrooms. For some time it was thought that a Viking settlement had been revealed. Eventually, however, the true significance of the find was understood: Skara Brae was nothing less than a Neolithic village which had flourished for about 600 years, from about 3100 to 2500 BC. It then remained unnoticed for a further 4000 years before its protective disguise was finally stripped away by the wind.

The excellently preserved settlement was larger than that at Knap of Howar, probably more closely resembling early Jarlshof in size. The method of house construction on all three sites is quite similar. The eight buildings of Skara Brae are all surprisingly uniform in design, like a Neolithic housing estate. They now lie in an exposed position close to the shore, although – like those at Knap of Howar – when they were built they were some distance from the coast, perhaps even separated from the sea by a small fresh-water loch.

To modern eyes the most unusual features of Skara Brae are its compactness and its subterranean situation. The site is more of a warren than a village, and when all the buildings were roofed it must have been difficult to detect from a distance, particularly in snowy weather. It is unlikely that this positioning was a

Skara Brae, Orkney, the most complete ancient settlement in the British Isles. It was discovered in the middle of the nineteenth century when a storm blew away its protective covering of sand.

deliberate attempt at camouflage, but a commonsense way of ensuring strong walls and maximum shelter from the elements. (Interestingly, in looking for ways to make houses as energy-efficient as possible, some twentieth-century architects advocate a return to underground dwellings.) Skara Brae's close-knit complex of houses is set in a midden. A number of dark and narrow tunnels link the womb-like burrows with each other and with the world outside. It has often been observed that the effect is similar to that of contemporary chambered tombs, such as those at Camster in the Highland Region, in which the lofty burial chamber contrasts sharply with its tiny entrance passage. Such graves were clearly intended as houses for the dead. It is tempting to consider the Skara Brae houses as man-made caves, as if their builders were confidently improving on the best that nature could provide – the architectural equivalent of the change from a hunter-gatherer to an agricultural economy. Nevertheless, the inward-looking settlement at Skara Brae still exudes a deep insecurity. Like frightened children, the homesteads cling together for comfort in an unpredictable and hostile environment.

Each square house, measuring up to six and a half metres across, has dry stone walls with a narrow and low doorway leading into the arterial tunnel. The entrances were originally fitted with wooden doors, whose draw-bar slots can be seen in the jambs. We cannot be certain how the structures were roofed, although the coverings were likely to have been similar to those outlined for the buildings at Knap of Howar. It is possible that for some religious or superstitious reason the whole site was systematically filled in at the time of its final abandonment.

One of the delightful aspects of Skara Brae is the wealth of internal detail surviving within each house. There are small alcoves in the walls, some intended for storage and others, to judge by their stone drains, serving as lavatories and outlets for slops. Other features include stone shelves and seats, a clearly defined hearth in the centre of the floor, and unexplained stone tanks, set into the ground and sealed with clay to make them water-tight. These may have served as receptacles for drinking water, live shellfish, or even as curing boxes. Couches or beds flank the walls on either side of the fire, and in the smaller, earlier houses they are laid in recesses. It is assumed that the hard bases were padded with heather or straw and bedecked above with canopies of fur. Comfortable though they undoubtedly were, these beds could not have held more than one sleeper – a surprising feature if one considers that for physical and emotional warmth double occupancy would have been a good deal more pleasureable. There can have been little privacy in the Skara Brae community. Apart from such general, rather obvious inferences, however, there is little more we can safely deduce about the social customs of its inhabitants. There is no way of telling, for example, whether property was held in common, or whether we are dealing with a monogamous or polygamous society.

The building known as House Eight, standing apart on the western side of the site, differs significantly from the others. Less regular in shape, it is without water tank, beds and shelving. Flint chippings on the floor and evidence from the smaller of the two buildings at Knap of Howar suggest that House Eight may have been a barn, workshop or communal kitchen. Excavations have revealed traces of similar buildings in the vicinity.

Neolithic Society

It is not only the buildings at Skara Brae which are important. The site has also provided archaeologists with a wealth of significant finds which, taken together with discoveries made elsewhere, allow us to build up a reasonably accurate picture of the technology of the period. The most common domestic find is pottery, the earliest pieces being plain and bag-shaped, probably in imitation of leather buckets or woven baskets already in use. They were toughened by baking in peat fires. Later pots were lipped and decorated with simple linear or cord patterns – the Grooved Ware found at Skara Brae is like that being used all over Britain at the time.

A late Neolithic pot found in Kintyre.
Utensils in this distinctive style are known as Beacharra ware.

The degree of isolation experienced by Neolithic communities is hard to estimate. We may infer from the uniformity of pottery design and the presence in Scotland of axes fashioned from English stone that a fairly extensive network of communications existed throughout the island, but we do not know how often people ventured far afield or how they made long journeys. It is safe to assume that water travel was common, for not only did settlers reach Britain by crossing from the Continent and then find their way swiftly to the most distant islands, but they must have done so in vessels of some size and seaworthiness. The domesticated animals whose remains have been identified were not indigenous to Britain, and so must have been transported over long distances by sea. It was

The central pillars of the impressive facade of the Neolithic chambered cairn known as Cairnholy I, Dumfries and Galloway. The original grave can be seen behind the uprights.

Cairnholy II, Dumfries and Galloway. Over the years the stones of the cairn have been taken for building, leaving the slab-built tomb standing starkly against the sky.

The original burial chamber of Cairnholy I. It was once covered with a cairn of boulders. The second chamber and range of standing stones were added later.

not necessary to import full-grown beasts, of course, but any ship capable of carrying calves, piglets, lambs and bags of seedcorn, as well as its crew, must have been several metres long. The types of craft most likely to have been used were either dug-out canoes or large coracles. The presence of cod bones at Knap of Howar indicates that fishermen sailed several miles out to sea in order to secure the most appetizing catches.

Other surviving domestic articles include jet clothing fasteners, bone pins, whalebone mallets and a variety of stone utensils such as scrapers and knives. From the number of tools obviously designed for woodworking, it is apparent that carpentry was well developed, though few of its products have survived. Planks were made, and we can guess from the way stone was cut and shaped that wooden joinery had been discovered. By far the most common tool was the stone axe, used for anything from felling trees to killing wild animals. An enormous variety of Neolithic axes has been found in Scotland, ranging from native implements to specimens in the attractive jadeite stone, imported all the way from the Alps. An 'axe factory' from about 2500 BC has been identified at Killin, Perthshire. Suitably-shaped pieces of stone, roughly carved, were sent from here to destinations all over the country where they were honed and polished locally into finished articles. As in Mesolithic times, flint was less commonly used in Scotland than in England, although it produced the sharpest cutting edges. Along with axes, other popular stone manufactures included adzes, sickles and arrowheads. Some of the larger communities may have developed a system of specialisation of labour, a few individuals spending their time working as carpenters, fishers or stoneworkers.

From archaeological evidence obtained at Isbister and at other British sites a few extrapolations can be made about the more personal aspects of life at this time. Though slightly shorter of stature, men and women appeared much as they do today. Their lives spanned no more than about 30 years, by which time they had invariably become wracked with the pain of poorly-healed fractures, abscesses and osteoarthritis, a common ailment in prehistoric times. It was rare for someone to survive to the age of 40 or 50. Those who lived that long were unquestionably highly regarded as valuable repositories of wisdom and custom (like living reference books in a pre-literate society). They must also have been revered as precious links with ancestors long since departed. It is unlikely that anyone dwelt in what we would regard as comfort, but since they knew no better there is little point in spending time on the more sordid aspects of their abbreviated existences.

The monoliths of the 'Twelve Apostles' stone circle have lain amid the fields of Nithsdale for over 4000 years. Only one of the original twelve is missing.

Camster Round Cairn, Highland Region, sits like an alien flying saucer on the rain-washed landscape.

Unlettered though it almost certainly was (we cannot be sure of the function of the linear patterns discovered on some stones at Skara Brae), Neolithic society had a clear appreciation of art and beautiful things. Beads and pendants for human adornment are plentiful. Some pottery designs are charming, and one or two items of rare delight have survived, such as decorated balls, mace heads and other painstakingly carved pieces of stone. The finest craftsmanship, however, was generally reserved for larger artefacts of more profound significance.

Cairns and Charnel Houses

The many hundreds of Neolithic tombs scattered throughout Scotland number among Europe's oldest pieces of indigenous architecture. While some are merely jumbled cairns, barely recognisable as human handiwork, others are profoundly impressive and evocative monuments to a civilisation long passed. Remarkable though this collection of ancient tombs is, however, it can distort our appreciation of the period, for it suggests a society obsessed with death. Death, burial and associated rituals obviously meant a great deal, undoubtedly more than in modern western society, for example. Yet the survival of many more tombs than, say, boats or houses does not necessarily reflect the comparative importance of these objects to contemporaries. A crude parallel may be drawn with early medieval Britain: we do not assume that war and religion were all that mattered then, simply because castles, cathedrals, monasteries and churches are virtually the only buildings to survive.

Ancient stone monuments are particularly difficult to date. Many were modified in the course of the centuries, and design varied from region to region. Furthermore, the timing of their construction and alteration does not always fit exactly with the neat stages (such as 'Neolithic' or 'Bronze Age') employed by prehistorians. For example, the first stone circles and henges (banked circular enclosures) appeared in Scotland towards the end of what is technically still the Neolithic period, though for the sake of clarity they are dealt with in the next chapter. Even so, a number of useful generalisations can be made about Scotland's remarkable array of early funerary monuments.

Apart from the less popular earthen barrows covering wooden mortuaries, the earliest tombs (built between about 4000 and 2000 BC) consist of stone chambers approached from the outside along narrow, low tunnels, with the whole construction hidden beneath a shaped cairn of stones. Within this basic pattern there is considerable variety. On Orkney, for example, we find tombs known as the Maes Howe type, named after the grand chambered cairn west of Kirkwall. One of the finest pieces of Neolithic workmanship in Europe, Maes Howe comprises a huge cairn (now roofed in concrete) on the summit of a flattened knoll surrounded by a ditch and bank. When it was built the tomb closely resembled contemporary stone houses, being about four and a half metres square with three raised alcoves set into the walls. Unlike domestic buildings, however, the tapering and buttressed ceiling rose to a considerable height above the floor: perhaps as much as four and a half metres. It represents thousands of hours of skilled work and must surely have been erected in memory of an individual, family or group of great significance.

At the other end of the country, in Galloway, the less grand but equally striking funerary monuments known as Cairnholy I and II represent a different approach to honouring the dead. Here the burial chambers are much smaller and built of solid slabs. Both tombs contain an inner chamber, permanently sealed from the one next to it by a huge flat stone. Cairnholy II is memorable for its elevated position on a hillside above the broad waters of Wigtown Bay, a site that led later generations to revere it as the final resting place of Galdus, a mythical early king of Scotland. The outstanding feature of Cairnholy I is the sweeping facade of standing stones which flanks the entrance to the graves. Though the columns are now fractured and sadly leaning, they still lend an awful majesty to the site.

Western Scotland had its own distinctive design of chambered tomb, known to archaeologists as the Clyde Cairn. The chamber was built of upright slabs, sometimes overlain with walling to give greater height. The best example of this type of structure is Nether Largie South, the earliest of a string of ancient monuments running along the floor of the Kilmartin valley in Argyll. Other well-known examples of chambered cairns include the Clava Cairns near Inverness, and the splendidly presented pair of burial mounds known as the Grey Cairns of Camster in Caithness. Camster Long Cairn lies in the shape of a stretched weasel skin above two tombs, one of which is divided into three sections by vertical slabs. Its sister Round Cairn covers a single passage and grave. The nearby (in Higland terms) Cairn O' Get also has a divided burial chamber. Neither of these tombs can compare with the remarkable stalled chamber at Midhowe on Rousay, which is sliced into no fewer than twelve separate compartments.

There is no uniformity about the positioning of Neolithic chambered cairns. Some were built on high ground, others in valleys (but apparently not on the best agricultural land), where they may have served as boundary markers. It is possible that clusters of tombs on Orkney were intended to represent whole communities of the dead, set apart from the living but inextricably interlinked with the same landscape as them.

Excavated tombs have provided fascinating yet tantalizingly incomplete insights into the values and customs of their builders. The most interesting revelation is that the burial places were not intended for single individuals, but for many people over hundreds of years. It was sometimes necessary to clear old bones from a charnel house before there was room for new ones to be deposited. This practice may explain the partial skeletons which are a feature of many sites.

Despite the fact that the bones of men, women and children have all been uncovered, it is unlikely that everyone merited having their mortal remains laid in a special monument. By examining the 150 skeletons found at the Orcadian chambered tomb of Quanterness, scientists have revealed that excarnation was practised: dead bodies were left until all the flesh had fallen from the bones (either with the gruesome help of primitive undertakers or simply by leaving the exposed corpse to be cleaned by natural depredation), before all or some of the bones were deposited in the local grave. This custom is another possible explanation for the incomplete skeletons. Cremation was also employed in some areas: fragments of charred human bone were uncovered in an arc of shallow pits on Lothian's towering Cairnpapple Hill, for example. Fire may also have played a key part in burial ritual, if we interpret correctly the charcoal found in the six hearths before the entrance to Cairnholy I.

Bones are not the only objects found within early funerary monuments. It is difficult to know what to make of the bizarre collection of relics with which people, whole or partial, were laid to rest, and since many graves were broken into long before they were methodically examined by archaeologists, many larger and more interesting objects may have vanished for ever. Pieces of broken pottery are common. The collection of fractured bowls taken from Unstan in Orkney was so distinctive as to give its name to a type of neatly decorated pottery: Unstan Ware. The sherds of a decorated bowl found in the outer charnel of Cairnholy I have been identified as belonging to a type more commonly found in England. The same grave produced a piece of coveted jadeite axe, alluding to the exalted status of one of its occupants. Other graves have revealed the remains of various creatures, both domestic (such as dogs) and wild (such as deer, fish and sea-eagles). The great birds may have had totemic significance.

What deductions about Neolithic society can be made from the evidence of funerary monuments? There was some form of ancestor worship. The scale of the works necessitated a considerable degree of co-operation between relatively large numbers of people at a time when the total population of Scotland was certainly no more than 10,000. This implies an organised society, perhaps arranged in hierarchical fashion. More than that it is unwise to infer. Nevertheless, if all the tangible and consequential evidence is pieced together one can arrive at a reasonably satisfactory impression of life in Scotland between four and six thousand years ago. Sadly, the gaps occupy more space than the picture itself, though this does not detract from the fascination of the flawed composition which remains.

3

BEAKERS AND BRONZE

Continental Influences

CONSIDERABLE CHANGES occurred in British society towards the close of the third millennium BC. Many of these were the result of influences spreading from the Continent, and so affected the north of the island rather later than the south. Nevertheless, within a few hundred years the civilisation of Neolithic Scotland had been radically transformed. Some scholars have spoken of a time of crisis, when there was a slight but noticeable cooling of the climate and when warfare became more common. They infer that society became more hierarchical and individualistic, and perhaps more superstitious, with greater attention paid to prestige and material wealth. Others take a less dramatic view of the situation, preferring to emphasise the gradual nature of the changes and rejecting the view that there was any significant increase in aggression and materialism. Clearly a good deal more work will have to be done before we are in a position to understand exactly what was going on, but it does now seem that, in the northern part of Scotland at least, the second interpretation accords more closely with the known facts than the first.

The physical manifestations of the changes take many forms. Communal burial chambers were often permanently sealed. Cremation and individual tombs became more popular. Large numbers of henges and stone circles were constructed, some associated with funerary customs, others laid out for purely ritual practices. New styles of pottery (particularly beaker ware) and other artefacts were first imported, then manufactured locally. In some areas camps and enclosures were abandoned and woodland began to regenerate itself. One or two settlements seem to have been laid out for defence, with walls and palisades. The biggest single change, however, was the development of metalworking, initially in copper and gold, then in tougher bronze: for the first time we can identify weapons specifically designed for warfare, rather than hunters' tools which might be employed for other purposes should the need arise.

The Neolithic era ends just as it had begun, with an unsolved mystery. We are almost as unsure how beaker pottery and metalworking came to Britain, and the precise relationship between the two, as we are about the introduction of agriculture. Bell-beakers first made their appearance in southern Britain in about 2750 BC; the earliest copper daggers (triangular-bladed, with projecting tongues at the top to which hilts could be attached) about fifty years later. It is tempting, therefore, to infer that they were both introduced by the same people. Beakers were widely employed on the Continent early in the third millennium BC and it

A fine earthenware beaker of the type found in many Bronze Age graves. The cord decoration was created by tying thick string round the pot while the clay was still malleable.

used to be thought that the areas near south and east coasts, where the earliest examples of the new vessels were found, had been invaded by Beaker folk.

The sites where the delicate Continental pots have been discovered often reveal evidence of quite wide-ranging cultural changes, such as individual burial in narrow pits or stone cists. Some prehistorians have identified a new race of people in Britain at this time, one whose skeletons suggest that they were both taller and broader, with skulls of a different shape. The full-scale invasion theory

The unusual U-shaped setting of standing stones at Achavanich, Highland Region. The function and precise date of the monument remain a mystery, although it is thought to have been constructed during the Bronze Age for some religious purpose.

Looking like a Neolithic war cemetery, the Hill o' Many Staines (Caithness) may once have contained about 600 small stones, arranged in a fan shape. The extraordinary setting is one of Scotland's many unsolved prehistoric mysteries.

is now unfashionable, having been replaced by two alternative (or possibly overlapping) explanations for the development of the new culture. One posits a partial invasion by beaker-bearing folk, whose success was facilitated by their possession of metal weapons. The second rejects all idea of a power-backed migration, offering in its place the equally plausible idea that new techniques, manufactures and customs entered Britain as a result of acculturation, arising out of the constant cross-Channel intercourse which had flourished since the country had become an island. In support of this view it is pointed out that in some areas several customs normally associated with the Beaker people, such as single-grave burial, round barrows and the use of metal objects, predate the appearance of beakers themselves. Acculturation, rather than invasion, is certainly the manner in which most technological and social change made its way north into Scotland.

Craftsmen and Artists

No Bronze-Age domestic sites are as well preserved as Skara Brae. Stone-built oval dwellings of the second and third millennia BC have been identified at Jarlshof. They are not buried, as tended to be the earlier custom in the north, but freestanding with solid thick walls. The interiors were designed as a number of paved alcoves around a central space. House Three was later adapted as a workshop for the local bronzesmith. Such substantial houses were not the norm in later Neolithic and Bronze-Age times. If they were, then surely more would have survived. In the lowlands, where most people lived, the typical house probably resembled the circular wooden or stone huts excavated at Green Knowe and Standrop Rigg. One other interesting type of dwelling has been identified. At Northton, on the south-west tip of Harris, people lived in large excavated trenches, about eight metres long by four metres wide, roofed with an awning made from hides and timber. The damp and foul-smelling burrow was cheered by a large fire burning in a central hearth.

As in the previous 2000 years, the great majority of Bronze-Age people were employed in farming, working either in single farmsteads or in small villages. These are frequently found on terraces or platforms cut into the south-facing slopes of hillsides which are no longer cultivated owing to the harsher modern climate. Several Bronze-Age field patterns have been revealed, but we do not know what system of land holding was employed. The walled enclosures were irregular, often with heaps of cleared boulders at the edge. At the end of the period there is evidence that the area under cultivation was being reduced and farmers were moving from arable farming to stock rearing, a transition which is discussed more fully at the end of the chapter.

It is possible that in the larger communities high ranking individuals – outstanding warriors or chieftains – did not need to engage in routine agricultural labour, which was left to those of lower status. Once the technology of crafting objects out of metal had been mastered, then agricultural land was no longer the most highly-prized commodity. Hunting was widely practised and it is possible that among the better off it was undertaken as much for sport as out of necessity. Remains of harness show us that horse power was employed, but whether this was for drawing loads or riding we cannot be sure.

Drawing on evidence from Britain and north-western Europe, we can say with some certainty how people appeared during the era of beakers and bronze. Woven woollen cloth and leather were used in the manufacture of clothes. For those who possessed them, most shoes were simple envelopes of hide, laced and wrapped round with leather thongs. Wooden-soled clogs may have been worn and there is some evidence that boots or gaiters were available. Most people undoubtedly went barefoot. For both men and women there were a variety of tunics and skirts, fastened at the waist, with cloaks and rough shirt-like garments for the upper part of the body. Hair seems to have been worn long. Hats of some description were common. On the evidence of long pins found beneath their skulls, women may have wound their tresses on top of their heads.

Much of our information on clothing has to be inferred from fastenings, such as buttons, pins and clasps which have survived better than cloth and hide. Plenty of articles of adornment have also come down to us. These include gold earrings, bracelets and armlets, necklaces of jet and other stones, and broad, finely crafted golden collars (known as *lunulae*) which may have been symbols of rank. Since they are not found in graves, they were likely to have been passed on from one generation to the next as badges of office. The most intriguing pieces of Bronze-Age art are the mysterious rock carvings which can be seen in many parts of Scotland. Some clearly represent real objects, such as axes, the sun or footprints. In the Ri Cruin Cairn in the Kilmartin Valley, for example, the slab at the western end of the southernmost cist carries the impression of seven axes chipped into the inner face of the stone. They all face the same way but are of different sizes and in no apparent pattern. Their significance now eludes us – perhaps the person buried there had seven children or spouses?

Even more mysterious are the broad areas of living rock, usually on a roughly horizontal plane, cut with a variety of abstract designs. The most common shape is known as 'cup and ring' – a circular indentation surrounded by one or more concentric circles. All sorts of explanations for the composition have been put forward, including astronomical and sexual symbolism, and mere doodling. Other shapes include grids, rectangles, lines and spirals, like the double one on an upright stone at Temple Wood (Argyll). One of the most extraordinary displays covers two broad rock faces at Achnabreck in Argyll with what looks like a crude stone equivalent to a painting by Jackson Pollock.

Two further details help to enrich our understanding of life in Bronze-Age Scotland. One is the new interpretation of 'burnt mounds', such as that excavated at Liddle on Orkney. This consists of an oval hut with a water-tight stone-lined pit at its centre. The structure certainly served a culinary purpose – large joints of meat were boiled or roasted in the stone oven, a practice which implies a society accustomed to co-operative enterprises. The tank, empty or filled with water, was heated by filling it with hot stones. What has puzzled archaeologists is the presence of alcoves in the hut walls. It has recently been suggested that the kitchen hut doubled as a bath house, and that the recesses were used by bathers enjoying the luxury of a sauna in steam issuing from the central tub. If this were the case, then washing was probably done as part of a religious ritual rather than for purely hygienic reasons. Another practice in Bronze-Age Britain was trepanation – cutting away a round piece of the skull with a sharp knife in order to relieve pressure on the brain. This drastic surgery was undertaken to cure a number of complaints, from migraine to madness, and amazingly some patients were able to survive more than one operation.

As society became more sophisticated and complex, so a greater number of individuals in the more prosperous parts of the country were able to devote themselves to specialist tasks, such as mining, metalworking, carpentry, pottery and trading. The original imported beakers were made of fine red ware, waisted and often decorated all over with the impressions left by twisted cord. It was not long before British potters began to fashion beakers of their own, and a number of regional styles developed. From the evidence of mead found in an example discovered at Ashgrove in Fife, the beaker was the ancient equivalent of wine glass and may have accompanied the spread of a new, alcoholic drink. It is heartening to think that the vessels' delightful design was matched by the quality of their contents. Later Bronze-Age pottery, deprecatingly referred to simply as

The larger of the stone circles at Temple Wood (shown here) was for some reason covered with a cairn in the later Bronze Age. The complexity of the site makes it one of the most intriguing of Argyll's many ancient monuments.

'food vessels', comes in a variety of shapes, sizes and designs, but fails to recapture the aesthetic charm of the original beaker.

The outstanding development of the Bronze Age was, of course, metallurgy, a craft which those living in Scotland were in an excellent position to exploit owing to the presence there of copper and gold. The earliest metal objects were Continental imports, but before long native craftsmen were producing knives, axes and jewellery of their own. The technology developed in four stages. The first smiths used wood or stone hammers to beat pieces of malleable metal into shape. They then discovered that the task was much easier if the material was heated beforehand, making it softer and less liable to crack. Eventually, when the metal was heated to a very high temperature, it melted and could be poured into moulds. When a small quantity of tin (about 10 per cent) was added to molten copper, the resultant compound – bronze – was much harder than either of the two ingredients in their pure state, and could be honed to produced a fine cutting edge.

Casting was initially done in flat, open moulds of stone or clay, which produced rather crude tools, mostly axes. Later two half-moulds were used. These were fastened together then filled with molten metal. The most sophisticated casting, in use by the Middle Bronze Age (about 1550 BC), is known as the 'lost wax' process. The first stage was to cover a wax model of the desired artefact with clay, leaving a small hole at one end. The object was then baked to harden the clay, and the molten wax poured out of the aperture while the cast was still warm. Next, liquid bronze was poured into the mould through the opening. When the metal had solidified, the clay was broken away to reveal a near-perfect copy of the original wax model. The only problem with this technique was that each manufacture was unique, since the clay moulds could not be reused. To overcome this craftsmen turned later to bronze moulds, though if they were not careful this could lead to fusion between the mould and its contents.

Apart from ornaments, bronze was used to make a huge variety of tools and weapons. For domestic use there were knives, razors, chisels, sickles, pins and capacious cauldrons, the last offering cooks far greater scope in the way they prepared large joints of meat. Before panel beating developed into a fine art, broad sheets of metal had to be made up by riveting smaller plates together.

Metalwork produced a revolution in weaponry, most noticeable in the advances made in axe and spear design, and in the appearance of swords and shields. By the end of the period, effective socketed or flanged axe and spearheads were being cast. The finest examples seem to have been reserved for ceremonial rather than practical use. The work of native craftsmen, copying and adapting styles from the Continent, has been divided by specialists into distinct chronological phases which culminated in the innovative Ewart Park phase, marked by elegant long-bladed swords in the shape of a carp's tongue. Bronze shields were probably purely ornamental, for experiment has demonstrated that leather-faced wood offers far greater protection from sword and spear thrusts. It appears that well-crafted weapons were commonly given as votive offerings to the gods. In 1780, six bronze shields were discovered buried in a circle at Luggtonridge, Ayrshire, and many daggers and swords have been recovered from marshes, rivers and lochs where it is presumed they had been cast to appease the water spirits.

During the second and third millennia BC, metalworking led to an increase in trade within the British Isles, and between Britain and continental Europe. To

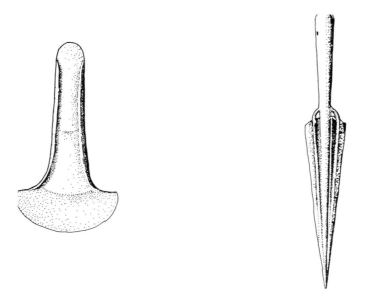

Bronze Age spear and axe heads. The introduction of metalworking in the late third century BC
transformed prehistoric craftsmanship.

When the chamber of the roofless Cairn o' Get was excavated in the last century, fragments of pottery, flint arrowheads and a quantity of bones (both animal and human) were uncovered. The site probably dates from the third millennium BC.

manufacture bronze in Scotland, for example, tin had to be brought from further south. Since there was no money, all commerce was conducted by exchange, which required goods and materials to be transported long distances. Where possible this was done by water, though the discovery of merchants' hoards (goods buried so that they did not have to be carried to a destination where they were not required) reveals that traders were also covering the length and breadth of the land on foot. There was also a flourishing trade in scrap metal.

Cists, Stones, Cairns and Circles

There is no clear dividing line between the funerary customs of the Neolithic and Bronze Ages. By about 2000 BC, however, chambered communal tombs had been finally sealed, sometimes using rites involving aspects of the new culture. The final ceremony at Cairnholy II, for example, involved the breaking of beaker pottery. There was much regional variation in burial tradition, and monuments first constructed in one period were frequently adapted to suit the requirements of later generations. Thus, at Nether Largie South, two Bronze-Age cists were added to the Neolithic chambered cairn. Furthermore, there is no clear distinction between tombs and constructions such as stone circles, which may not have been built primarily as funerary monuments. In the centre of the recumbent stone circle at Loanhead of Daviot in the Grampian Region traces of cremated child and adult bones were discovered among sherds and pieces of charcoal. Cists are architecturally less impressive than chambered tombs, though the presence in them of a number of gravegods makes them valuable sources of information about the time when they were being used.

One of the key points about chambered tombs, whatever their design, was that they were communal charnel houses which could be reopened to admit further human remains. They were gradually replaced – whether as a result of conquest or acculturation we cannot tell – by cist burials. A cist was essentially a short rectangular stone burial box (to call it a coffin would be to suggest something movable, which cists clearly were not) built to receive a single figure. It was covered with a cairn of stones. The slab walls, floor and lid of a cist were shaped with considerable care to ensure that they fitted together as snugly as possible. At Ri Cruin the stone side plates were cut with grooves to accommodate the end pieces, a technique which may have been copied from contemporary woodwork practice. The inhumed (buried without cremation) corpse was generally arranged in its cist in a foetal position, with the knees drawn up to the chest. This custom interests those with some knowledge of undertaking: since bodies rapidly stiffen after the moment of death, those for whom a cist burial was intended had to be persuaded to breathe their last doubled up, or somehow they had to be folded later. Whichever solution to the problem was employed, some rather macabre scenes may be imagined.

One or two deductions about society and belief in post-Neolithic society can be made from the practice of cist burial. It seems safe to assume that the change from multiple to single graves intimates that some individuals were now much more highly regarded than others. The beaker burial of a child, as at Cairnpapple (see below), suggests that status might be inherited and not just earned through action, indicating the acceptance of an hereditary ruling family or class. (The child may of course have been sacrificed, in which case the supposition is invalid.) The presence in cist graves of beakers and one or two other useful objects, and the arrangement of the body as if prepared for rebirth, surely means belief in an afterlife.

Changing prehistoric burial practice is best displayed in the arresting chain of cairns and other monuments lying along the floor of the Kilmartin Valley, where we have already noticed the Neolithic tomb of Nether Largie South. The shape of this cairn changed from oval to round when cist burials were placed on top of it during the second millennium BC. Neolithic cairns were not the only ones to be reused by Bronze-Age engineers eager to save labour and ensure that their patron's final resting place was certain to be propitious: the Bronze-Age Nether Largie Mid Cairn houses two cists, one added after the other had been sealed; three cists were uncovered at Ri Cruin; and even more at Glebe Cairn, which appears to have been reconstructed completely on several occasions. Although most burials were fashionable inhumations, the northern cist in Ri Cruin held cremated remains. Just to remind us how various and complex were the funerary customs of our distant ancestors, the nearby Temple Wood Stone Circles present a different way of honouring the dead, with cists (one found to contain a beaker) in and around a circle of stones and attendant cairn.

Cairnpapple displays in a single monument much the same sequence of change as at Kilmartin. The lofty cemetery, which commands a view right across the waist of the country from the Clyde to the Forth, began as a series of pits for cremated human remains. Then came an earthen circle, or henge, circumscribing the entire site. At some time a ring of standing stones and an obscure rectangular structure were placed within the henge. During the Beaker Period a small grave was dug near one of the standing stones and another in the middle of the site, replacing the original monument which stood there. The central grave was clearly that of someone important, for it sported a large upright stone and its own kerb of smaller stones. Several interesting objects were found within, including two beakers and a wooden club. Later still, another cairn was heaped upon that covering the beaker graves. It held a cist burial from the time when food vessels were the fashion. Afterwards the cairn was extended and two cremated burials (a custom that was coming back into fashion by about 1500 BC) were added. Finally, perhaps in the third or fourth century BC, four cist graves were dug between the cairn and the now much-reduced ditch.

The final stages of prehistoric work on Cairnpapple Hill make a good introduction to developments at the end of the Bronze Age. The return of cremation has been interpreted as a renaissance native culture in opposition to the Beaker customs which had prevailed for at least half a century. We do not know whether the resurgence, if indeed there was one, involved any political action. The complete absence of any funerary monuments in Scotland from the last centuries of the Bronze Age may be explained by events discussed at the end of the chapter.

Both Temple Wood and Cairnpapple introduce the relationship between ring cairns and stone circles. Standing stones, whether single, grouped or laid out in a definite pattern, are such a striking feature of the Scottish landscape that even the most casual tourist cannot fail to notice them. (It is worth remembering, too, that there were once many similar monuments in wood, all long since rotted away.) The precise function of these remarkable monoliths will always elude us, though it was certainly in some way religious rather than secular. It is most likely that they delineated places of particular holiness, making them the temples, churches or cathedrals of their day. This explains why they might be used as burial grounds, and ties in with the circular design of cup-and-ring marks.

Much interesting but misguided effort has been spent trying to prove that arrangements of prehistoric stones presupposed a sophisticated knowledge of astronomy and mathematics. There has been talk of a universal 'Megalithic Yard' of measurement and of stone circles being elementary calculators for making astronomical observations. Current thinking is that such claims are grossly exaggerated, particularly as over the course of some four thousand years the stones have weathered and settled, so altering their positions in relation to

The eerie grave preserved beneath the modern concrete dome atop Cairnpapple Hill (Lothian) is only one of the features which makes the site so memorable. The hilltop served as a burial ground and place of worship for thousands of years.

A pair of Iron Age graves on Cairnpapple Hill, the last in a long series of prehistoric monuments on the site.

heavenly bodies and each other. The most that can realistically be claimed for them is that some are situated with an eye to the position of the sun or moon, making them useful as calendars for timing rituals and regularising the seasons.

A wide range of religious stone monuments was erected in all parts of Scotland from late Neolithic times onwards. The most impressive and probably one of the oldest is that at Callanish on the Isle of Lewis, raised some 5000 years ago. Its appearance is literally like nothing else on earth: tall tongues of variegated stone protrude in the shape of a ragged cross along an uneven ridge above Loch Roag. Where the two lines meet they divide to form a circular brooch with a single upright at its centre. The longest branch, reaching to the north, is in two rows. It forms an ill-aligned avenue to the heart of the temple, where a small chambered cairn lies. From the circle the four arms of the cross extend approximately to the four points of the compass, the southerly being the most exactly orientated. The effort and organisation required by the tiny population of Lewis to set up such an extraordinary edifice are a telling indication of the strength of their beliefs.

More usual are rings of stones set within henges, circular or oval banks and ditches pierced with one or more entrances. The best-known examples are also on an island site: the Stenness Stones and the Ring of Brodgar on Orkney. Both are vast, ancient and incomplete. Brodgar, which originally comprised some 60 stones, is over 100 metres in diameter. Stenness is less than half that size and contained only 12 monoliths. Both monuments were built probably at the end of the third millennium BC. Smaller circles in good condition are the Torhouskie Stone Circle in Dumfries and Galloway, and Cullerie Standing Stones in Grampian. Two further stone configurations deserve a mention, the peculiar Hill O' Many Stanes and the unique U-shape of large stones at Achavanich, both on the east coast above Helmsdale. The former, now consisting of about 200 rocks the size of milestones but originally numbering as many as 600, is the best example of an arrangement found only in Caithness and Sutherland. Its purpose, like that of the Achavanich U, is a mystery. Smaller groups of stones abound. For example, there is a splendid trio of huge monoliths, one of which has fallen, in a field near the cup-and-ring carvings of Drumtroddan (Dumfries and Galloway). An impressive example of a single stone (four metres high and weighing many tonnes) can be seen near the obscure little cairn of Strontoiller in Argyll. Uncertain though the function of all these sites may be, the visitor cannot fail to marvel at the skill of primitive engineers who undertook such massive projects, each of which must have absorbed the resources of a small community for years.

No description of early stone circles would be complete without a mention of the examples where they accompany burial cairns. The celebrated Clava Cairns near Inverness have given their name to a group of similar structures found only in the surrounding region. There are three cairns at Clava, two of which contain chambered graves, approached down passages. The third is a ring cairn, with the grave opening from above. All three are surrounded by broadly-spaced rings of standing stones. Dating from the later third millennium BC, it has been suggested that they were shrines of a small group, such as a distinguished family.

Recumbent stone circles are so named because their pillars were arranged in ascending height towards the south-west, where a large stone (the recumbent) was laid on its side between two flankers. The clearest example, at Loanhead of Daviot in Grampian, surrounds a ring cairn bordered with an embedded kerb. The outer stones stood in small individual cairns, and traces of sherds and burned human bone have been discovered beneath the rocks of the large central cairn (now flattened). Finally, there is the singular configuration of stone circles at Temple Wood, to which we have already alluded. The broader circle surrounded an ancient burial place. It was later covered by a large cairn beneath which the remains of three cists have been located. Two were on the periphery, but one is still clearly visible in the centre of the monument.

Trauma and Change

The climatic changes experienced in our own day have made prehistorians much more sensitive to the effects of such fluctuations in the distant past. If a marked warming or cooling of the planet's surface can have a serious effect on a technologically sophisticated culture, capable of predicting and sometimes counteracting the vagaries of the weather, then how much greater must have been the impact of new temperature, rainfall and wind patterns on a primitive people, whose lives were so closely tied to the natural world. Modern scholarship suggests that the major social changes noticeable towards the end of the second millennium BC were not triggered by political developments but by a marked deterioration in the climate.

By about 1000 BC the British Isles were becoming wetter and cooler. In Scotland the change was exacerbated by massive volcanic activity on Iceland, which raised a dense blanket of dust over the surrounding seas and landmasses. The sun was blotted out for long periods, leading to a drop in atmospheric pressure and further heavy rainfall. The immediate repercussions of these dramatic developments on the inhabitants of the northern Britain can only be guessed at: we do not know what superstitious practices they turned to, what sacrifices they made and what prayers they offered to appease the gods who, in their anger, had plunged the landscape into a watery gloom. Longer-term effects of the cataclysm included the abandonment of marginal farmland in the face of advancing peat bog, the desertion of northern settlements and migration away from the inhospitable Highlands. This put pressure on those living further south, forcing them to take steps to defend themselves, their possessions and their lands. Wooden palisades were raised for the first time on Eildon Hill North in Lothian, and similar structures appeared in many neighbouring settlements. Scotland had entered the Age of the Fortress.

For all its remarkable achievements, Bronze-Age culture in Scotland was still comparatively primitive. It survived without the benefit of the wheel (except perhaps on a handful of ornamental carts) and without writing. It had no towns, no money and, as far as we can tell, no cross-country routes of communication we could call roads. Furthermore, it is reasonable to infer that its political and commercial systems must have been relatively small-scale and simple. Of course, this does not imply a barbaric society – indeed, it may be argued that it embraced a proclivity for pacifism which we would be wise to emulate. Perhaps when Man lives in uncrowded conditions close to the natural environment he does not feel it necessary to turn his aggressive instincts towards his own kind. The problem for students of this period is that we just do not know enough to substantiate such observations. As with previous periods, we can write only a shady social, cultural and economic history of the Bronze Age in Scotland. We lack names, either of individuals or of groups, and there is no record of significant specific events. In short, there is no politics.

The identifiable periods which we use to make the past more manageable are often as arbitrary as the national boundaries drawn on the map of Africa by nineteenth-century imperialists. They cannot take into account local differences and must perforce be seen as little more than useful generalisations. Technologically speaking, for example, Scotland remained in the Bronze Age until about 600 BC. But so great were the changes occurring there, as the world entered the last pre-Christian millennium, that they make an obvious point at which to take up the story afresh.

4

THE AGE OF
IRON

The Celts

THE CELTIC hero Cu Chulainn was endowed with the qualities of an ancient god:

> beautiful of face and figure, sharp-sighted, eloquent, wise, a talented swimmer and horseman, an expert board-game player and tactician, a skilled fighter and hunter, an aggressive destroyer and fearless plunderer in unknown territories.

Overblown though this description may be, it provides us with a powerful insight into the ideals of the culture which dominated Scotland for more than a thousand years.

The origins of the Celts are obscure. This paradoxical yet compellingly attractive race of people emerged gradually over many prehistoric centuries to appear as an identifiable European group in the first millennium BC. Tall, fair-haired and vigorous, their diffuse tribal society was noted for its creative brilliance, the unusually favourable position it afforded women and for its aggressive participation in war and raiding. The groups of horse-riding warriors who appeared in Britain in about 700 BC were accompanied by traders, metalworkers and artists. They had mastered the art of chariot construction and were experts at fortress building. Their craftsmen combined Classical, Eastern and Bronze-Age traditions into an intricate, varied and wholly new style of art, whose vital sophistication is one of the enduring delights of European culture.

The manner of the introduction of Celtic language and customs into Scotland is obscure and much disputed. We meet much the same problem as we did at the onset of the Neolithic and Bronze-Age periods: was there large-scale invasion by Continental tribes bearing new skills, or can the changes be explained by acculturation and the roughly simultaneous arrival of small bands of migrants? The most straightforward explanation is that from the seventh century onwards large numbers of Celts came to Britain, bringing with them their language, and knowledge of iron smelting, fort construction and other techniques which first appeared at about this time. This neat hypothesis has been challenged on several fronts. It has been argued that a version of the Celtic language spread to Scotland, along with other Indo-European tongues, in early Neolithic times. There is also evidence that there were at least two distinct phases of Celtic migration, one around 700 BC and a second three hundred years later. Current thinking suggests, therefore, that the Celticisation of Scotland was a gradual process, undertaken by small warrior bands over several hundred years and perhaps preceded several millennia earlier by a form of the Celtic language. A few groups may have crossed the North Sea directly to the fertile east coast, while the majority probably moved into Scotland from England, either seeking booty and fresh lands, or driven north by new waves of Continental invaders settling in southern Britain, as was the case in the first century BC. The native population was not obliterated, but reduced to a subservient status beneath the umbrella of a dominant Celtic culture.

The Celts usher in the final phase of British prehistory, known as the Iron Age. In England this period ran from about 700 BC to the Roman invasion of 43 AD. It is followed by the Roman era, and then, after about 400 AD, by the Dark Ages. Contemporary Scottish history defies such neat compartmentalisation, for no part of the country was ever occupied by the invader for long, and Roman ways had little impact above the line of Hadrian's Wall. Consequently, Celtic Iron-Age society flourished in Scotland well into the Christian era, resulting in considerable cultural overlap between the pre-Roman, Roman and post-Roman eras. The construction of brochs, for example, took place from some time in the middle of the first millennium BC to about 200 AD. For the sake of clarity, however, where possible discussion in this chapter will focus on the developments of the pre-Roman millennium.

Settlements and Strongholds

Unlike previous periods, the enduring monuments from the first millennium BC are strictly secular. For reasons which are not fully understood, no burial sites of any significance were constructed after about 1200 BC. It may be that the disruptions caused by the worsening weather conditions so impoverished and unsettled the exhausted inhabitants of Scotland that they were unable to concentrate sufficient resources over a long enough period to build elaborate monuments such as stone circles and burial cairns. Yet within a few centuries they were sufficiently well organised and motivated to throw up massive strongholds of stone, earth and timber. So we probably need to look elsewhere for an explanation for what occurred. Perhaps there was a change in religious belief during the prolonged time of troubles? As the rains fell continually from darkened skies, previously fertile fields turned to unproductive marsh and once-flourishing settlements were abandoned to the hostile elements, the men and women of the later Bronze Age may have felt that their ancestors, the planets, or whatever else they had placed their faith in, had let them down badly. After all, the Biblical flood may have confirmed Noah in his faith, but it hardly endeared those left behind to the old man's capricious deity. There is evidence that during the first millennium BC water acquired religious significance: no doubt it was seen as an element worth appeasing.

Only after an interval of about a thousand years is there evidence of a return to the practice of inhumation. The Iron-Age cists added to Cairnpapple Hill have already been noted. Stone-lined graves have been found near the hillfort at Broxmouth near Dunbar and aerial photography has identified what appear to be Iron-Age burial mounds in Angus. But the great majority of human bodies from the later Bronze Age and Iron Age have simply disappeared. Skeletons buried intact would have been uncovered. All kinds of suggestions, therefore, have been made as to what happened to them, including cremation followed by a scattering of the ashes, and exposure of the corpse (on rocks or even on housetops) until, after the flesh had rotted or been picked from the bones, the skeleton was somehow disposed of.

It is not always easy to distinguish the ordinary dwelling places of this period from fortified settlements. Several sites (such as Hownam Rings, Roxburgh) appear to have been adapted over the centuries as circumstances changed, and for

'Cup and ring' carvings on rocks at Drumtroddan, Dumfries and Galloway: representations of solar bodies, or simply the work of a doodling shepherd? The significance of the weird markings still eludes us.

A re-creation of an Iron Age pallisaded settlement, showing the type of circular hut common in Scotland for at least two thousand years.

reasons of prestige some farms took on the appearance of fortlets. The great bulk of the population was engaged in farming and lived in round houses, either sited singly or gathered in small nucleated settlements near their fields and grazing areas. In southerly areas the walls of dwellings were of timber or woven wattle and daub, usually resting on stone foundations. Further north, where wood was much scarcer, walls were of dry stone construction, about a metre thick and some one and a half metres high. The large conical roofs, resting on well-crafted wooden frames and supported in the middle by tall posts, were covered with thatch, hides or turf. Some houses were of a considerable size, the largest examples being almost 20 metres in diameter. Because of the height of the walls, there was insufficient room to stand upright near the outer rims of the buildings, so these areas could be used only for storage or sleeping. The single doorways were low and could be entered only by stooping – a feature which put unwanted intruders at the mercy of those inside. The small entrances and the absence of windows made the interiors rather dark and smokey, though they were also warm, snug and comparatively secure. Floors were paved with flat stones upon which a covering of straw or rushes was laid. In some houses attempts were made to sweeten the rather unsavoury atmosphere by strewing the ground underfoot with herbs. It is difficult to reconstruct the insides of these round houses precisely, for evidence of partitions and other wooden fixtures has long since rotted away.

In several parts of Scotland the remains of elaborate larders, known as earth-houses or souterrains, have been discovered. As with so many other prehistoric structures, the precise function of these underground shelters is something of a mystery. On the mainland they were essentially banana-shaped trenches, sunk into the earth beside a dwelling and roofed at ground level with stone, or turf over a timber frame. The walls were stone-lined, making them ideal cool storage places for grain, dairy produce and other perishable foodstuffs. Their design varies in different parts of the country. In some places the tunnel ends in a small chamber; in others, such as the fine example at Carlungie (Angus), there are side passages. Some led directly from within an adjacent house, others had separate entrances. They vary in size from small cellars to cavernous stone-pillared store rooms capable of holding far more than would ever be required by a single family. The latter might have been granaries for storing the tribute demanded by Roman overlords. Whatever their function, experts are fairly sure that outside Orkney and Shetland earth-houses served no function other than storage: they were not hides or tombs. The underground workings at Rennibister on Orkney and at Jarlshof on Shetland, on the other hand, were probably built with different purposes in mind. The long, narrow design of the passages makes them difficult to enter, and the discovery of human bones in the chamber at Rennibister indicates that the building may have been used as a tomb, a refuge, a prison – or even as a place of more sinister interment.

Another interesting development was the crannog, a house built on an artificial platform some distance from the shore of a loch, marsh or estuary. Despite the obvious difficulties of constructing such island homesteads, they were popular from at least the early Iron Age until well into the Roman period and beyond. Evidence suggests that some were still in use in the seventeenth century. The advantage of this type of dwelling was not simply that it offered

Culsh souterrain (Grampian), believed to have been built in about 200 AD as a cool storehouse for farm produce.

excellent protection against incidental attack by both Man and beast. It was also comparatively pest-free, and combined a dwelling place with a convenient fishing platform. To judge from their postions near good arable land, most crannogs were inhabited by farmers.

The first stage in crannog construction was to choose a natural feature on the bed of the site, such as an outcrop or raised rock just beneath the surface, upon which to anchor the foundations. Obviously it was important to select a position which required a minimum of additional work. Where the water was too deep or the floor of the loch too unstable to support the full width of the dwelling, a platform of large logs was laid. Later this was gradually reinforced with boulders to make it more substantial. In several lochs the remains of these platforms can still be seen protruding as small rocky islets, as is the case with the wooded Ardanaiseig Crannog in Loch Awe.

Crannog houses were essentially the same as those on dry land: circular with low walls and conical roofs. The platform running round the outside of the dwelling was sometimes extended to form one or more jetties. The wooden causeway linking the settlement to the mainland could be burned or pulled down when danger threatened.

From the seventh century BC onwards, when Celtic influence was first making itself felt in southern Scotland, it became common to render settlements more secure by surrounding them with ramparts. This development, coupled with the increasing number of weapons being manufactured at the time, tells us that society was becoming more aggressive and warlike. (It also reflects on the passivity of previous millennia, when only one stronghold of any consequence – Meldon Bridge – has been found.) Defensive walls were of timber, earth or stone construction and in some instances comprised several concentric rings of defence around a central enclosure. Among the better-known examples are Craigmarloch Wood (Renfrew), Harehope (Peebles), and the fortified farm near Whithorn, known as Rispain Camp. Here, a large rectangular earthen bank was surmounted by a strong timber stockade, pierced by a single fortified gateway. The enclosure held a number of circular wooden huts where the community lived in self-sufficient comfort and secure prosperity.

In the south and east of Scotland the most spectacular Iron Age monuments are hillforts. The name 'hillfort' is somewhat confusing, however, because many of these spectacular constructions were usually much more than strongholds. Sites such as Traprain Law and Eildon Hill North, for example, were not just refuges but permanent settlements and important centres of local administration – the first Scottish towns. Unfortunately only from the air can their true shape and scale be appreciated. There are few places where the uninitiated foot traveller is able to get a clear understanding of what the original fort looked like, for the grand walls which once stood so strikingly around many southern crests are now mostly reduced either to untidy cairns or to gentle, heather-strewn undulations along the hillside.

There is no distinct dividing line between an enclosure surrounded by a wooden palisade and a hillfort furnished with earthen ramparts and stockades of timber and stone. Castlelaw (Midlothian) began as an oval enclosure protected by a simple wooden wall. A rampart was added later and the defences were further strengthened shortly before the arrival of Roman troops in Scotland. The position of the fort is interesting as it is overlooked by higher ground. The site's vulnerability has been taken as evidence that defence was only one, and perhaps not even the most important, of the place's several functions.

Unlike their English counterparts, the great majority of Scottish hillforts had stone walls. On a number of sites the building rocks were interspersed with timber to increase the structure's strength and stability. The wooden walls of some forts rested on stone foundations. In others beams were laid either vertically or horizontally between layers of rocks. The idea of lacing stone walls with timber came from Germany and may well have been a Celtic import. It has given rise to vitrified stonework, a phenomenon which has exercised the minds of prehistorians over many years. It seems that on occasion the reinforcing beams within a stone wall were set on fire. When this happened the timbers could act as chimneys within the stonework, enabling the conflagration to reach very high temperatures. Where the surrounding stonework contained a high proportion of silica, at a temperature of between 700° and 1200° centigrade the stones melted and fused together in a process known as vitrification. The best-known example of this is at Finavon in Angus. As the strong, slippery surface of a vitrified wall could be an additional part of a fort's defences, in some places experiments in deliberate vitrification may have been conducted. In most cases, however, firing was undoubtedly the result of assault.

As with castles of the medieval period, the weakest point in a hillfort's defences was the entrance. Consequently most forts had no more than two points of access, each defended by an elaborate system of gateways and ramparts which made it impossible to enter in a straight line. The exceptional number of gateways into Brown Caterthun (Angus) has been explained as a much later modification, added when the hill was used as some kind of medieval commercial centre. A few Scottish forts, such as Cademuir and Dreva Craig, used the defensive device known as a *chevaux de frise*. This consisted of many pointed stones, each about a foot high, placed close to each other in the ground beyond the walls on the more vulnerable slopes of the hill. The resulting obstruction, looking like a miniature version of the defences erected against tanks during the Second World War, would have been effective against horses and chariots, and would also have served to break up a charge by footsoldiers.

A hillfort's principal defences were the concentric rings of walls and ditches which formed a virtually impregnable barrier around the central enclosure. A visit to White Caterthun probably gives the best impression of how grand one of the larger hillforts must have appeared: though the mighty double walls (the inner of which once stood three metres high and no less than twelve metres thick) are now no more than lines of tumbled boulders, the commanding position and majestic strength of the stronghold can still be appreciated. It is an awesome monument to the skill, perseverance and organisational ability of Scotland's Iron Age inhabitants.

In its prime, the hillfort on Eildon Hill North was even more impressive. Within its triple ramparts, over a mile in circumference, there stood a small town of some 2000 inhabitants housed in 300 wooden huts. We know very little about how such a community was organised, but it goes without saying that a settlement this size could not have survived without a complex system of local government to provide food and water, settle disputes and arrange matters such as waste disposal, building and the division of labour. Classical sources suggest that Celtic society was not strongly hierarchical, land and goods being held in common and leaders elected from among the tribe. In troubled times the hillfort served as a place of refuge, where all those living in the area could seek sanctuary until the danger passed. Sieges were uncommon. Normally the town acted as a commercial and administrative headquarters. The evidence of such sophistication surely dispels any impression gathered from classical sources that the civilisation of Iron Age Scotland can be dismissed as 'primitive'.

In the north and west of the country, a rather different tradition of fortification emerged. Here, the population was smaller and more widely scattered, so there was little need for large hillforts. Their place was taken by duns and brochs, stone-built strongholds designed to shelter no more than a couple of dozen people with

The rocky slopes of Dreva Craig (Borders Region) were once the site of an impressive Iron-Age fort defended by two stone walls and, on one flank, a series of projecting upright stones, known as a chevaux de frise. These were intended to break up the charges of assailants.

their possessions and livestock. Though there are low-lying and island examples, a dun was usually a circular or oval fortlet frequently built atop a craggy knoll, whose precipitous sides added to the position's strength. The site usually determined the dun's extent and shape. Dun Lagaidh in Highland Region is typical, holding the highest point of a steep-sided ridge beside Loch Broom and commanding remarkable views over the water to Ullapool. Watched over by the dun above, farmland stretches on either hand along the shore of the loch.

Most duns were little more than fortified farmsteads. They were built near fertile soil, with timber farm buildings, freestanding huts or lean-to sheds within the enclosure. The dry stone walls themselves, commonly punctured with single entrances, were quite low (about three metres) but had to be at least five metres thick in order to support even such a modest elevation. The problem of how to gain height using this method of construction, without making the lower sections of wall impossibly broad, was eventually overcome by building two parallel walls. The presence of numerous duns along the west coast of Scotland suggests that throughout the Iron Age people of the region lived in small, isolated agricultural communities, where sporadic raiding was endemic. We know little about how they ordered their day-to-day lives, though it may well be that the traditional Highland culture, which lasted until the eighteenth century, has its roots in this period.

Brochs are Scotland's unique contribution to advanced prehistoric architecture. Occurring only sporadically in the southern part of the country, they were built in large numbers in the Western and Northern Isles, and Caithness. They were truly magnificent structures, huge tapering towers of unmortared stone rising some nine metres above the ground, and displaying an elegance and grandeur unmatched by any contemporary native structure. For over 1000 years, until the appearance of the first stone castles, they were the most impressive pieces of architecture in Scotland.

Not all the 500 brochs were built to exactly the same pattern, though they had certain basic features in common. They were round and double-skinned, with single low entrances set at the foot of the battered (i.e. splaying towards the base) and windowless walls. One of the most obvious design differences can be seen at ground level, where archaeologists distinguish between ground-galleried and solid-based styles. The former, found largely in the Western Isles, have hollow walls from the base upwards. The latter were built on an undivided foundation in which small cells were sometimes left. Entrance passages run through the

A storeroom set within the massive five-metre thick walls of Edinshall (or Odinshall) Broch near Preston in the Borders Region. With a diameter of almost 17 metres, when intact this rare Votadini broch must have dominated the landscape for miles around.

The well-preserved broch of Dun Dornaigil, or Dun Dornadilla, stands in the remote heart of Sutherland beside the River Strathmore. Because the refuge was built on sloping terrain, the architect had to make the north-western face much taller than the others.

A view of Dun Telve, showing clearly the broch's double-skinned construction and the large flat stones which linked the two walls. Note the gaps in the inner wall on the left to reduce the weight above the doorway.

thickness of the walls, with rooms interpreted as guard chambers let into the sides, as at Dun Telve. The lintel over the doorway, like the fine triangular piece at Dun Dornaigil in Sutherland, is often the largest single stone in the broch. Heavy wooden doors separated the interior of the building from the outside, and the jambs against which they closed can still be seen, together with the slots left to accommodate timber draw-bars. The long flat stones needed to bond the inner and outer walls also provided galleries within the cavity – at Mousa (Shetland), the finest surviving example of a broch although perhaps not the most typical, there were five galleries linked by a stairway climbing all the way to the wallhead. For some reason the stairs in other brochs stop short of the top of the building. In order to let light and air into the galleries (and to lessen the weight of the walls, particularly over the entrance passage) openings were left at intervals in the inner wall.

Another feature common to all brochs still standing to a reasonable height are the 'scarcements' for supporting intermediate timber constructions within the building. Sometimes the scarcements are in the form of jutting stones; in other brochs they are ledges set back into the stonework. Many brochs were not roofed over completely but had thatched wooden galleries following the inside curve of the wall, with a space in the centre left open to the sky. Brochs built in this pattern would have been less dark and stuffy than the fully-roofed versions, but in wet weather there must have been problems with cooking and drainage. To judge from the evidence of Mousa, which still stands to almost its original height, brochs were provided with some form of walkway round the top of the walls. This was used as a look-out post and, when the occasion demanded, as a fighting platform.

It is much easier to say what brochs were than why, when or by whom they were built. Current thinking is that they probably first emerged in Orkney in the middle of the first millennium BC, the result of years of experimentation with different types of stone wall construction. They are likely to have been refuges rather than permanent dwellings, for as far as we can tell they were just one – albeit by far the largest – of a number of buildings in the neighbourhood. Their coastal positioning suggests that it was from the sea that danger was most likely to come, perhaps in the form of raiding parties seeking slaves. A stout broch could have had a deterrent effect too. If there were softer targets in the vicinity, no slaver would wish to set about attacking one of these towers, whose walls must have been virtually impregnable to an assault party armed only with hand-held weapons. There is hardly any evidence of a broch having been destroyed as a result of aggressive action, and surprisingly few pieces of military equipment have been found in the surrounding villages. Thus it seems reasonable to assume that brochs were built for both prestige and practical purposes – by hiring an itinerant specialist in broch technology a community could purchase respect and, more importantly, long-lasting security.

Excavations conducted near a number of brochs, notably Guerness and Midhowe on Orkney and Clickhimin on Shetland, have provided quite detailed insights into the societies which thrived in the shadows of these formidable strongholds. The culture appears as a fascinating blend of the developments which had occurred over the previous 6000 years. Hunting, fishing and fowling are represented by the bones of deer, cod and wild duck. Stone implements such as hammers and querns for grinding were still being used, as were implements carved from antlers and pieces of bone, including those scavenged from stranded whales. Stone lamps are another interesting find.

Farming was obviously crucial to the economy, as we can deduce from the discovery of large numbers of bones of domestic animals (largely sheep, cattle and pigs). Corn was harvested and local wool woven into coarse cloth. The pottery made on site was rough but serviceable. Bronze was still being cast, largely to make ornaments, while quantities of slag point to a flourishing iron industry. Bone dice provide a pleasant human touch to what is otherwise a rather humdrum collection of artefacts. Most illuminating of all are articles which have clearly been imported from afar. Pottery and a bronze ladle, both of Roman origin, were uncovered at Midhowe; the dig at Clickhimin revealed a piece of glass from a dish similar to those being made in Alexandria in the first century AD. These finds counteract inferences, easily made from the defensive posture of the brochs, that northern society was inward-looking and isolated.

Change and Continuity

Our survey of the settlements and structures of Iron Age Scotland has already touched upon several aspects of everyday life of the time. Further generalisations can be made with reasonable safety, though differences are apparent between the north-west and the remainder of the country. The semi-urban culture of a hillfort such as Eildon Hill North cannot have resembled very closely that of the Guerness settlement. Confusion over the precise nature of regional differences is not helped by the fact that much of our understanding of Celtic society derives from information provided by Greek and Roman writers, whose evidence was drawn largely from the Continent.

In southern Scotland during the first millennium BC, the rather attractive egalitarianism, which seems to have been a hallmark of several primitive cultures, was starting to break down. Tribal groupings appear: the Novantae, Selgovae and Votadini in the south, the Damnonii, Epidii and Venicones in central Scotland, and in the Highland and Grampian Regions a galaxy of smaller groupings who, for the sake of convenience, may be lumped together under the general heading 'Caledonii'. Each nation was likely to have been headed by a class of nobles, from whose ranks a monarch or chieftain – sometimes a woman – was drawn. The bard, whose function was a curious combination of entertainer, newscaster and historian, was another enjoying privileged status. In England, a defined social hierarchy emerged, extending down through the ranks of priests, craftsmen and farmers to mere slaves, and it is possible that a similar change took place where the population was comparatively dense in southern Scotland. Nevertheless, it is much more likely that throughout most of the country kinship remained the principal social bonding.

During the Celtic era the potter's wheel was introduced and metal working, particularly weapon manufacture, was widespread. Many of the more charming artefacts from this period found in Scotland were made elsewhere. Foreign designs were easily copied, however, and continued to influence native art for many centuries. As we have seen when looking at burials, religious observance remains obscure. It may well be that the rather unpleasant Druidic rites practised on the Continent and in southern Britain were also followed in Scotland. These included ritual human sacrifice, which enabled the officiating priest to foretell future events by studying the contortions of the dying victim. Was this the fate meted out to the twelve-year-old boy whose remains were found buried in four pits alongside the bodies of cows and sheep on South Uist? Having been killed by a stab in the back, his skeleton was quartered when all the flesh had rotted away from the bones.

It was generally agreed at the time that the Celts were a most handsome race: tall, usually fair-haired and muscular. They were proud of their appearance and regarded it a disgrace to grow fat, something which it must have been hard to avoid for the few who lived to middle age, for the Celts were renowned as heavy drinkers. They paid particular attention to their coiffure: moustaches were fashionable for men, and hair was worn long (Boudicca's fell to her knees) and swept back off the forehead. It was frequently washed, dyed and stiffened, so that the description of Cu Chulainn's perfect locks gives the impression of an early punk:

> His hair curled round his head like a red hawthorn bush used to plug a hole in a hedge. If a heavily-laden apple tree had been shaken above him, not one piece of fruit would have reached the ground – all of it would have been impaled on the spikes of his hair.

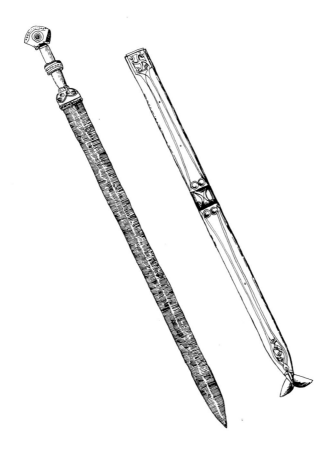

The level of skilled workmanship achieved in the Iron Age can be seen clearly in this sword and scabbard. Early Celtic styles of decoration link directly with the art of Dark Age Pictish craftsmen.

Both sexes dressed in tunics, heavy cloaks fastened with a brooch, and leather shoes. Men wore patterned trousers tied at the ankle. For battle some may have removed all their clothes (which they also did when playing a form of hockey, known as *baire*) and painted their bodies, though this is unlikely to have been the custom of those fortunate enough to have owned one of the chainmail surcoats which were being made at the end of the period. Much more is known about the Celts than about those who preceded them – they were expert musicians and keen games players, for example – but since much of the evidence is of a later date or refers to Continental practice, it is perhaps unwise to speculate further on exactly how they lived in Scotland.

As we have seen, during the centuries immediately prior to the Roman invasion there were signs of a clear distinction between the hillfort society of southern Scotland and the broch builders of the north and west. For a time during the first two centuries AD this division became more pronounced, as the lower part of the country came temporarily under the influence of the conqueror. But even here the lively Celtic Iron-Age culture of the pre-Christian centuries was never seriously threatened. When the Roman troops finally withdrew at the end of the fourth century, the traditional native customs and practices rapidly reasserted themselves over the whole country.

5

5

ROMANS AND CALEDONIANS

The Influence of Rome

WITH THE arrival of the Romans in Britain, we move from prehistory into history. We also meet the beginnings of a tradition, which was to endure into the Middle Ages and beyond, that the people of northern Britain were distinct, separate and independent. The Roman historian Tacitus, who accompanied Agricola on his Scottish campaign towards the end of the first century AD, puts into the mouth of the Caledonian leader Calgacus (the first Scotsman known to us by name) the earliest expression of what might be termed Scottish nationalism. Before the battle of *Mons Graupius* Calgacus reminded his troops:

> We are the cream of British manhood. Until now we have remained in hiding, not even casting our eyes on the advancing tyranny. Shielded by nature, we are the men of the edge of the world – the last of the free . . . .
> Britons are being sold into Roman slavery every day . . . and it is we who are next on the list to be taken. When that happens, there will be nothing left we can call our own: neither farmland, nor mines nor ports. Even our bravery will count against us, for the imperialists dislike that sort of spirit in a subject people . . . . Therefore, as we cannot hope for mercy, we must take up arms for what we cherish most . . . . We will be fighting for our freedom . . . so when the two armies meet let's show the invader what calibre of man Caledonia has kept up her sleeve.

The words and possibly some of the sentiments are entirely fictitious, the product of a fertile imagination and a singular literary tradition. They are nevertheless a

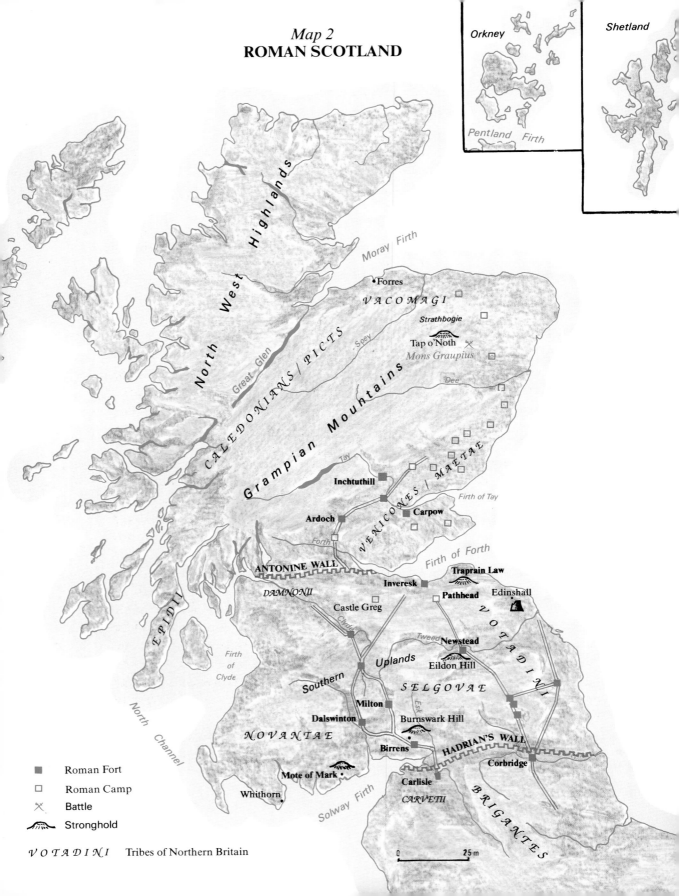

Map 2
ROMAN SCOTLAND

Orkney

Shetland

Pentland   Firth

Moray Firth

• Forres

V A C O M A G I

Strathbogie

Tap o'Noth ✕
Mons Graupius

Spey

Dee

North West Highlands

Great Glen

C A L E D O N I A N S / P I C T S

Grampian Mountains

Tay

Inchtuthill

V E N I C O N E S / M A E T A E

Firth of Tay

Ardoch

Carpow

Forth

ANTONINE WALL

DAMNONII

Inveresk

Traprain Law

Pathhead

Edinshall

Firth of Forth

V O T A D I N I

Castle Greg

E P I D I I

Clyde

Southern

Uplands

Tweed

Newstead

Eildon Hill

S E L G O V A E

*Firth
of
Clyde*

Milton

Dalswinton

Esk

Burnswark Hill

N O V A N T A E

Birrens

HADRIAN'S WALL

North Channel

Mote of Mark •

Corbridge

Whithorn •

Carlisle

CARVETII

B R I G A N T E S

Solway Firth

■   Roman Fort

□   Roman Camp

✕   Battle

🌄   Stronghold

V O T A D I N I   Tribes of Northern Britain

0   25 m

valuable contemporary insight into the assumed reaction of the Celtic people of Scotland to the arrival of a Roman army in their midst.

It was not what the Romans did in Scotland so much as what they failed to do that proved significant in the long run. A land frontier was much less satisfactory than a coastal one, and there is little doubt that once Agricola's fleet had confirmed that Britain was an island the invaders would have liked to extend their sway over the whole of it. Only when resistance had been crushed and the blanket of Roman civilisation, with its law, urbanisation, roads and attendant wealth, spread from the south coast to Sutherland could the conquerors have afforded to relax, and reduce the expensive forces of occupation. But this was never to be. Britannia remained a heavily garrisoned outpost of empire, the Roman south permanently divided from the barbarian north by a broad and troubled no man's land. The division thus established was by no means immutable – when the imperial power withdrew, its walls and forts soon fell into disrepair, and the warring tribes and petty kingdoms of the Dark Ages felt little compunction to adhere to the frontiers of a bygone time. The legacy of Rome, however, was not lost entirely. The efforts of the would-be conquerors had shown just how difficult it was for a government based in the south permanently to control the rugged territory above the Tweed, and in attempting to do so they forced a temporary unity among the peoples of the north which was one day to re-emerge. The Romans certainly did not create Scotland, but they demonstrated the possibility that a separate Scottish nation might one day exist.

Archaeological evidence indicates that the tribes of northern Britain had very little direct contact with Rome before the invasion of AD 43. This does not mean, of course, that they were wholly ignorant of the mighty power which was gradually extending its power towards them – no doubt they had met with slaving parties seeking human merchandise to sell in imperial markets, and there must have been awe-inspiring travellers' tales, much distorted in the telling, of the conqueror's military prowess, ruthlessness and fabulous wealth. The relative isolation of the peoples then inhabiting Scotland might have been an advantage when it came to resisting the invader. They had little time or opportunity to be undermined by the chimerical advantages of living under Roman rule: the prosperity, and much-vaunted security of the Pax Romana. Instead, as we read in the words which Tacitus gave to Calgacus, they saw the Romans as the true barbarians, who murdered, robbed and raped in the name of law, who reduced a land to a desert and called it peace.

The territory immediately below the present border between England and Scotland, later divided by the construction of Hadrian's Wall, belonged to the Brigantes, one of the most numerous of the ancient British tribes. In the area above this, marked by the Tyne-Tees line in the south and the Forth-Clyde isthmus in the north, lived four groupings: the Votadini in the east, the Novantae in the west, in the present Dumfries and Galloway Region, and the Selgovae between the two, controlling a large swathe of southern Scotland from Eskdale to the Forth, with the Eildon Hills as their headquarters. The territory of the Damnonii included most of the triangle of land between the Forth-Clyde and Highland lines. Above this stretched the vast mountainous domain of the Caledonians, the Epidii, the Maetae and other Highland tribes. On occasion the name Caledonii is used rather indiscriminately by Roman commentators to describe all northern groupings. It is important to bear in mind that the sources for these tribal divisions are Roman, and that consequently they appear much more orderly than they really were. As has been suggested, one of the chief effects of Roman invasion was to bring about coalitions of small and disparate groups of settlers to resist the invader. There were few distinct political frontiers in pre-Roman Scotland, and Caledonia in particular was little more than a convenient geographical expression. However, lest we underestimate the effectiveness of these federations of primitive people, many of whom enjoyed a somewhat curious amalgam of Iron and Bronze-Age cultures, it is worth remembering that for centuries they proved capable of the most surprising resistance, harassing and occasionally embarrassing the greatest military power in the western world.

Agricola

Twenty-five years after their invasion forces had landed on the shores of Kent, the Romans controlled all the southern part of the country except for Wales. The first commander to push north towards Scotland was Petillius Cerialis, who in AD 71 took advantage of a breakdown in the Romans' agreement with the Brigantes to move against them and advance as far as Carlisle. After the recall of Cerialis in AD 74, there was a pause in Roman expansion until the appointment in AD 78 of Gnaeus Julius Agricola as Governor of the Province of Britain. Agricola was no stranger to the country, having already won respect here when in command of the Twentieth Legion. Though the campaigning season was drawing to a close when he arrived, he immediately made his presence felt by subduing those parts of Wales which had lain beyond Roman control. The next year he turned his attention to the Brigantes, bringing them to heel and consolidating Cerialis' work by moving up the west coast to the Lake District and Solway Firth. That winter he planned the most daring Roman campaign in Britain since the invasion, 37 years previously.

Agricola's advance in AD 80 took the form of a pincer movement. While the Ninth Legion marched up the eastern route to Inveresk on the Firth of Forth via Corbridge and Newstead, thereby separating the Selgovae from the Votadini, the Twentieth Legion followed a westerly route from Carlisle towards the same destination, slicing between the Selgovae and the Novantae. The combined force then marched north to the Tay, meeting with little resistance. The operation was brilliantly executed, not only in the way the two armies synchronised their movements but also in the manner in which the accompanying fleet was used to supply them and prepare for their arrival by harrying the countryside ahead. The next year was spent consolidating the extensive gains by building a chain of small forts across the Forth-Clyde line and securing the territory to the south with fortified bases and a network of roads. It has sometimes been assumed that the northerly bases were later accommodated into the Antonine Wall, though there is little evidence for this. The large forts at Dalswinton, north of Dumfries, and Newstead, adjacent to the Eildon peaks, together with smaller Roman bases to the north and south, ensured that the Selgovae and Votadini were isolated and their resistance broken. This freed Agricola to tackle the Novantae.

In AD 82, Agricola crossed the Solway and marched west across Dumfries and Galloway to southern Ayrshire, establishing bases as he went. He may at this point have considered crossing to Ireland, for it seemed a soft target and there would have been much prestige in adding an entire island to the empire. For some reason, however, he decided against the move and concentrated instead on the conquest of northern Britain. With this aim in mind he sent a reconnaissance fleet up the west coast of Scotland to ascertain whether there was an easy route in that direction round the formidable obstacle of the Highlands. When his captains reported back that the terrain to the north was even less hospitable than that on the east coast, he was in a position to prepare for his final assault. It was probably already quite clear to him that he could not easily hold his new northern frontier as long as the Highland tribes, the Caledonians and others, remained unvanquished. Moreover, in order to provision their Scottish garrisons it was

The elaborate earthworks of the huge Roman fort at Ardoch enclose an area of almost two hectares. The size of the stronghold and the complexity of the defences indicate that it was a key point in the network of roads and fortified bases with which the Romans tried to hold down the troublesome tribes of northern Britain.

Grassy undulations are all that remain of most Roman forts in Scotland. Though the ramparts of the small fortlet of Castle Greg in Lothian Region are particularly well preserved, it is now difficult to envisage the busy camp as it once stood.

necessary for the Romans to dominate Fife, the fertile garden of Scotland. This task would be much easier once the Caledonian threat had been removed. It is likely, too, that Agricola's spies had information of a planned attack on the weak defensive line that had been thrown up between the Forth and Clyde. Thus the principal aim of the Roman commander was to draw the Caledonians into open battle and crush them before they moved south.

The campaigns of AD 83–4 were conducted in the same manner as those of the previous years, with the army's advance covered by a powerful fleet. First, Agricola divided his forces, a tactic which almost led to disaster when the Ninth Legion found itself subjected to a devastating night attack. Under the cover of darkness, the Britons slew the sentries and burst into the legion's camp. Only the timely arrival of Agricola himself saved the day for the Romans, and the enemy were driven off into the hills. For all its apparent lack of military sophistication, the foe clearly could not be underestimated.

Having wintered on the Tay, the next spring Agricola pushed on to the north, hoping to provoke the enemy to attack. One has only to compare the Roman army with the forces opposing it to understand the immense advantages which the former would have in battle, even if the Caledonians selected a site favourable to themselves. The Roman army was a superb fighting machine. At its heart were the self-sufficient legions of 5000 Roman infantrymen: professional, heavily-armoured soldiers whose training enabled them to operate deep in hostile territory and fight under virtually any conditions. Drawn from all over the empire but never stationed near their homeland where there might be a conflict of loyalties, the legionaries were bound together by loyalty to Rome and a fierce pride in their unit. Their remarkable success all over Europe and the Middle East was due not only to the highest standards expected of each individual soldier but by the excellent support services attached to each unit: engineers, medical staff, a supply corps and administrators. During his campaign along the east coast of Scotland, Agricola chose to hold his legions in reserve, placing auxiliaries in the front line of battle and keeping his crack troops back in case of emergency. After a long period of campaigning he probably felt that he could trust his hardened second-line troops in all but the most perilous situations. Moreover, a legionary was an expensive item, the product of years of careful training and therefore not something to risk losing from a chance arrow or spear-thrust in exchanges with mere barbarians. Though primarily an infantry force, the flexibility of a Roman army was increased by the presence of cavalry units capable of launching devastating charges and taking out enemy chariots.

The Celtic Caledonians, though no doubt sturdy and fearless fighters, were no match for the professional legions of Rome. The northern tribes had no training in large-scale combat, which meant that they were incapable of any subtle manoeuvres of battle tactics. The men were lightly armed, fighting half-naked, largely without body armour and equipped with swords and any other weapons they could lay their hands on. Their most feared troops were the charioteers, drawn from among the highest ranks in society. But while a charge of densely packed, wheel-knived chariots could be crucial on a level, lowland battlefield, among the rock-strewn glens of the Highlands they could prove more of a handicap than an asset. In the light of the differences between the two sides, Calgacus 'the swordsman', leader of the motley band of Caledonians, would have been well advised to follow the strategy of the previous couple of years, harassing and shadowing the enemy but refusing to meet them in pitched battle. But he must have been under some pressure to justify the summons which had been sent out among the scattered farmsteads and villages of the north, calling all men to take up arms and unite to destroy the invader. Such people could ill afford to be away from home for long. They came expecting battle and when no decisive action was forthcoming they must soon have grown restless and begun to drift back into the hills. Calgacus knew that sooner or later he had to confront the Romans or lose the confidence of his men.

The Roman army advanced methodically up the coastal plain, keeping in touch with the fleet and digging in each night behind the turf walls and palisades of a marching camp. It is from the remains of these temporary fortifications, situated a day's march apart, that archaeologists have been able to gather most about the movements of the Romans in Scotland. The longer the invaders' supply lines became, the more confident Calgacus must have felt, and when after passing Stonehaven the Romans struck inland towards the north-west he must have believed that his moment had come. Gathering his forces in Strathbogie, he patiently awaited the arrival of the enemy. The long-expected battle was to be fought at last.

For Agricola the move inland may have been a calculated gamble. Had he stuck to the coast, the Caledonians might well have kept their distance until their forces had melted away, any chance of battle going with them. Although this would have left Agricola master of the eastern Highlands, he could never have felt safe there until the natives of the district had been broken and hostages taken as guarantees of future good behaviour. Thus, by making directly for the Moray Firth through the hills of Garioch and Strathbogie, the Roman commander was laying down a challenge to Calgacus which the native general found impossible to resist.

The site of the battle of *Mons Graupius* has long been disputed. It is almost certainly in the region of Huntly, probably on the hill now known as Bennachie. Here the Caledonians arranged their 30,000-strong army with the chariots drawn up on the lower slopes, and wisely waited for the Roman assault. The tactic was not dissimilar to that employed by the English at Hastings almost a thousand years later, and was equally unsuccessful.

After each side had attempted to unsettle the other with a barrage of assorted missiles – arrows, spears and stones – Agricola personally led his auxiliary foot soldiers in a frontal attack upon the Caledonian lines. While this gruesome hand-to-hand fighting was going on, part of the Roman cavalry engaged the enemy chariots, destroying them completely before turning to assist the infantry. At this point the remaining Caledonian forces swept down the slope, apparently hoping to outflank their enemy. The simple manoeuvre was thwarted by a charge from the remaining Roman cavalry, which rode through the enemy ranks, wheeled about and attacked the foe in the rear. There followed a fearful slaughter of the tribesmen, at the end of which some 10,000 of their number lay dead upon the battlefield. The Romans are reckoned to have lost a mere 360 men out of a total of 30,000.

Mons Graupius was indeed a significant Roman victory, but it is unwise to liken it to the defeat of the Jacobites at Culloden, as some writers have done. The latter was fought with Scots on either side and led to a total subjugation of the Highlands. At *Mons Graupius* the Caledonians had been defeated but not broken, as the southern tribes had been by earlier campaigns. After the battle two-thirds of the defeated army had escaped, disappearing overnight into the mountains from where resistance to the invader could be continued.

Nevertheless, for the moment Agricola's triumph was complete, and he proceeded north to the land of the Borestii (probably around Forres). Since the season was already late, he then decided to call a halt to campaigning for the year. His immediate aim appears to have been to consolidate his gains in north Britain by building a large legionary headquarters at Inchtuthil on the Tay and isolating the Highland region with forts to the north-east and south-west of it, blocking the entrances to the glens. This would enable him to put further pressure on the area, whose dispirited inhabitants had already received a sharp lesson about what resistance to Rome could mean, in order to bring about its eventual submission.

Agricola probably regarded his victory over the Caledonians as an important step towards the complete conquest of northern Britain. Just as he had prefaced his move into the Highlands by sending his fleet on a reconnaissance trip up the west coast, he now dispatched the ships on a circumnavigation of Scotland. The voyage demonstrated beyond doubt that Britain was an island. But Agricola may have found rather depressing the extent and nature of the territory still left outside Roman control.

The Lessons of War

As it turned out, the battle of *Mons Graupius* marked the high point of Roman power in Britain. The next year Agricola was recalled to Rome, a routine matter since he had already exceeded the time normally spent as governor of the province. His successor, Sallustius Lucullus, maintained the northern policy as far as circumstances would allow, but he was never in a position to attempt anything more than containment. In AD 86, imperial demands led to the withdrawal of a legion from Britain, leaving the new governor with insufficient troops to man the base at Inchtuthil, let alone launch another major assault on the north. Over the next few years the Romans engaged in a gradual but definite withdrawal from Scotland, destroying their forts as they went. They were to return to the region on several subsequent occasions, making forays up the east coast very similar to that pioneered by Agricola, but they were never able to get a permanent grip on the area. For better or worse, the Caledonians and their northern neighbours (many of whom were later subsumed within the general term 'Picts') never came under the sway of Rome.

By the end of the first century AD, the Roman move south seems to have turned from a planned withdrawal into a retreat. The garrison town of Inchtuthil, with its proposed array of 64 barracks, medical centre and drill-hall, all contained within a stone wall 1800 metres long, was abandoned in AD 87, before it had been completed. Watchtowers north of this were manned until about AD 90, after which they too were allowed to fall into enemy hands. Five years later, the Caledonians and their allies had secured the site of Ardoch, which the Romans had strengthened only a few years previously. After this the native warriors gathered confidence, quickening the pace of their advance and attacking Roman bases directly rather than waiting for them to be relinquished by the hard-pressed foe. In other words, a war of attrition had become one of aggression. Of all the forts in southern Scotland which fell into British hands at this time, only Milton appears to have been voluntarily surrendered. The others, including the mighty strongholds at Dalswinton, Newstead and Birrens, fell to direct assault. By about AD 105 the Romans had been pushed back to the line of the road known as Stanegate, running from the Tyne to the Solway Firth. Although the present boundary between England and Scotland was not settled for another 1500 years, it is curious how often before this a line drawn east or north-east from the mouth of the River Esk has served as a significant political frontier.

The success of the people of north Britain in driving the Romans from Scottish territory is a reflection not only on the temporary weakness of the invader but also on the strength and thinking of those who were able to take advantage of the new situation. It seems as if the lessons of *Mons Graupius* had been well learned. The fact that at first the Romans withdrew under pressure suggests that they had been subjected to consistent and effective harassment, probably in the form of ambushes on the road and sudden, violent raids upon insecure garrisons already weakened by a shortage of provisions. It is extremely unlikely that the Britons followed any sort of master plan or overall strategy, but their ability to assemble, arm and supply large numbers of men at a single point means that their forces were rather more than random gatherings of disaffected tribesmen eager for the spoils of war.

The period of British expansion ended with the accession of Hadrian to the imperial title in AD 117. The new emperor visited Britain on several occasions and it was after one such trip in AD 122 that he decided the best way of settling the problem of the northern frontier was to construct a gigantic barrier right across the country, dividing the bulk of the Brigantes from their potential allies further north, the Selgovae and Novantae. The idea of a walled frontier was not new – Hadrian had seen such devices employed successfully elsewhere in the empire – but the scale of the British enterprise was to exceed by far anything so far attempted.

The construction of Hadrian's Wall, as the barrier has come to be known, was a stupendous task. Though its design was changed during the building to rectify mistakes in the original plans, and major alterations were made over the succeeding centuries, the wall was a magnificent feat of engineering. It remains the outstanding Roman monument in Britain and one of the finest in the whole

An artist's impression of how a milecastle on Hadrian's Wall might have looked. As the period of Roman occupation drew to a close, the discipline among the garrisons was relaxed and buildings like these served as barracks for soldiers and their families.

empire. To pass it by because it lies outside modern Scotland would be a pointless semantic exercise. If it is reasonable to distinguish at all between Scotland and England during the Roman period, then Hadrian's Wall is the obvious line along which to make the division.

As originally planned, the wall was to have been merely a raised platform north of the garrisons strung out between the Tyne and the Solway, a sentry-walk rather than an impermeable barrier. This idea was scrapped in favour of a continuous fortified curtain, erected between about AD 122 and AD 128. When

This view of one of the best preserved and dramatic stretches of Hadrian's Wall illustrates how the builders utilised natural features (in this case a steep scarp) to increase its defensive potential. For much of its life, however, the barrier served more as a base for controlling the zone above it than as an impregnable frontier.

A reconstruction of the great hall excavated at Balbridie. Though put up in Neolithic times, it probably resembles a type of structure in use for thousands of years.

first built, the wall was of stone in the east, some three metres thick and four metres high, and of turf at its western end, thicker and lower. The latter section was later rebuilt in stone. There were garrison milecastles every thousand paces (the Roman mile) with two turrets evenly spaced between them. At their western end the fortifications were continued along the southern bank of the Solway Firth to prevent an outflanking attack across the estuary.

Later modifications included moving the garrisons up to the wall itself, where they were housed in large forts such as Chesters and Housesteads, and digging a huge earthen rampart to the rear of the wall. The function of this 'vallum', which consisted of an unbroken ditch almost six metres wide and three metres deep with massive mounds on either side, has been the source of much puzzlement. Current thinking is that it delineated the southern limit of a military zone into which strangers were not welcome. It also provided a means of communication between the forts along the wall (a road ran between the ditch and the northern mound), and served as a substantial barrier against attack from the rear. It is worth pointing out that in the event of the wall being breached the vallum would have made a dangerous obstacle in the path of the retreating garrison – clearly the Romans did not contemplate withdrawal from such an expensive and elaborate fortification.

Unlike the Berlin Wall of our own century, Hadrian's Wall did not mark a sharp division between two cultures. Roman military commanders knew only too well that depth and flexibility were the keys to successful defence. For much of its history, therefore, Hadrian's Wall served as a sort of *ne plus ultra*, a line of final defence before which Roman influence extended into southern Scotland. Indeed, within a few years of its construction the wall was being seen more as a springboard for further conquest than as a purely defensive structure.

If the Selgovae and their neighbours had been alarmed at the appearance of Hadrian's Wall, the fact that it had been thought necessary to build such a barrier was in some ways a testimony to their strength. For a while it left them masters of their own territory, free to organise raids on construction parties and, later, on the wall itself. Impressive though the new structure was, it signified that the first round in the fight between the Romans and the people of north Britain had been a draw.

The status quo was shattered in 138, when Governor Lollius Urbius marched north in strength from the wall, seeking to reoccupy in the name of Emperor Antonius Pius the territory lost to Rome 40 years previously. Details of the campaign are not known, but it is clear that within seven years he had succeeded in establishing Roman power in most of the areas once controlled by Agricola. The two routes north, roughly along the paths of the present A74 and A68, were re-established and the Roman forts rebuilt. It has been convincingly argued that the appearance of British conscripts (probably from the Selgovae and Novantae) in the Roman army in Germany at this time demonstrates a complete subjugation of those tribes. Ardoch became a Roman base once more and further forts were built above the Firth of Forth, particularly in the direction of Fife. Most remarkable of all, however, was the decision to build another wall.

The Antonine Wall, which ran from the Forth to the Clyde, was a shorter and cheaper version of that built further south. It was of turf construction on a stone base, with more forts and twice as many troops per mile as Hadrian's Wall. The new wall's turf construction, which means that it does not survive in anywhere near such good order as Hadrian's Wall, and the fact that much of it has disappeared beneath urban development, have led to it being viewed as something of a poor relation. The fortification across the waist of Scotland was in fact another tremendous achievement of Roman engineering. It was no mere temporary fortification, for once it had been completed the gates were removed from the milecastles on Hadrian's Wall and causeways were constructed over the vallum at regular intervals.

The history of Romano–British relations in the second half of the second and early years of the third century is extremely confused. Part of the problem is that Roman literature of the period does not always distinguish clearly between the Antonine and Hadrianic Walls, making it very difficult to work out precisely where military operations were taking place. All that we can safely say is that there was an angry boiling among the tribes of northern Britain, resulting in open rebellion against the Roman overlords and assaults on their strongholds. As at the end of the previous century, it appears that the conqueror had cast his net too wide: when he attempted to draw it in, it broke under the strain. At times the problem was exacerbated by internal strife within the empire.

Disaffection involved all the tribes of northern Britain, including the Brigantes. On occasion both walls were abandoned and later reoccupied, though it is possible that Roman troops effected a permanent evacuation of the Antonine Wall as early as the 160s. The line's remote position and lengthy supply lines, coupled with the fact that it could easily be turned by a seaborne operation, must have made it a strategic liability. For quite long periods the Romans may have resorted to paying subsidies to the tribes bordering their areas of occupation, buying their clientage and thereby establishing a buffer zone against further encroachment. This system broke down late in the second century when a confederacy from Strathmore, known as the Maetae, joined with the Caledonians and Brigantes to drive the Romans from Scottish territory yet again. Their success was shortlived, however, for in 197 the Emperor Severus made Virius Lupus Governor of Britain and dispatched him thither to restore Roman rule in the province.

By 208 Hadrian's Wall had been restored and prepared as a base for bringing the people of the north to heel. At about this time Emperor Septimus Severus arrived in Britain with his sons Caracella and Geta, determined to move north in order to punish the Caledonians and their allies and discourage them from further raids. An expedition set out from Carpow in Fife in 209 and progressed as far as Moray, following much the same path and employing tactics similar to those of Agricola. There is no record of the Caledonian leader Argentocoxos (or, intriguingly, 'Silver Leg') attempting to face the invader in the field, and the natives were obliged to accept humiliating terms of surrender. This provoked a fresh British revolt in 210, leading to a second punitive campaign of particular ferocity in which Severus' son, Caracella, was ordered to slaughter every Briton his army came across. After this, Caracella imposed terms upon the Caledonians and Maetae, who by this time were unlikely to have been in any position to strike a hard bargain, and returned south. Brutal though they may have been, the expeditions of Severus and Caracella clearly had the desired effect. Henceforward, as far as we can tell, Roman and north Briton co-existed in relative harmony for almost a century. The settlement was a practical compromise. The imperial power was undoubtedly master, and even though direct Roman rule now stopped at Hadrian's Wall, its influence continued to be felt throughout the buffer zone to the north of it. Nevertheless, Rome's status in Scotland depended very much on it not exercising its authority too strongly.

6

INDOMITABLE
BARBARIANS

Beyond the Wall

A S MAY already be suspected, there is a powerful temptation to write a lopsided history of Scotland during the Roman period. This arises because the only literary sources are the works of classical historians, which understandably concentrate on the activities of their own people rather than those of their enemies. They also tend to speak rather disparagingly about those living outside the empire, except on those occasions when barbarian strengths are exaggerated in order to magnify the achievements of those who overcame them. Thus a political history of Scotland at this time can become the story of Roman attempts to subdue the country rather than one of resistance and internal development. There is a similar danger in social, cultural and economic affairs, which may focus too much on the extent to which native society was influenced by outside forces. Though a Romano-centric approach might have some justification when dealing with the first two centuries AD, a period dominated by the struggles between north Britain and the invader, once the Antonine Wall had been finally abandoned it is feasible to discuss the area above Hadrian's Wall (particularly north of the Forth-Clyde line) as a quite distinct and separate entity.

Roman influence on Scotland was patchy, often short-lived and, except perhaps in areas immediately adjacent to the border, of little enduring social or cultural consequence. We have already noted the only political change which affected virtually all the tribes of north Britain: the coalescence of peoples into larger units in order to resist the invader more effectively, and later to challenge his supremacy. By the time of the Severan campaigns in the early part of the third century we are told that the peoples living above the Forth-Clyde line had merged into two tribes, the 'greatest people' (the Caledonians and the Maetae) having absorbed all lesser groups.

The far north and west were least touched by the imperial power. Trade certainly increased during the early centuries of the new millennium and the recovery of Roman artefacts from many coastal sites suggests that even those living in the remoter corners of the British Isles must have been aware of developments further south. It is reasonable to assume, therefore, that this completed the change from Bronze-Age to Iron-Age culture, which hitherto had been proceeding only unevenly in isolated areas. Otherwise, life went on much as it had done before the arrival of the legions.

Preoccupied with the problems of where the design for brochs originated, who built them and for what purpose, specialists have tended to steer round the equally perplexing question of why, from the second century onwards, they fell out of use. The most obvious answer is that in more settled times such elaborate refuges were no longer needed. If this was the case, we have little idea what the threat was which had now receded, and it is surprising that duns do not appear to have suffered a similar obsolescence. The erection of isolated brochs outside the agglomeration in the north and west is equally mystifying. How, for example, can we explain the presence of the huge second-century broch at Edinshall, in the heart of the territory of the Votadini? Was it the work of an itinerant northern expert, hired by a local magnate after the Roman withdrawal in the latter half of the century?

The abandonment of brochs coincides fairly exactly with the appearance on Shetland and in the Western Isles of a new form of dwelling, the wheelhouse. These structures appear to have been a northern elaboration of the more common roundhouse, a regional solution to the problem of building in areas where there was a shortage of suitable construction timber. In wheelhouses the stone roof pillars serve also as partition walls, a neat piece of architectural lateral thinking. Like the spokes of a wheel, they radiate from an open space in the centre of the building to form small separate chambers.

As far as we can tell, the civilisation of the Caledonians and Maetae – who from the fourth century onwards appear under the collective title of Picts – was that of the Celtic Iron Age, outlined in chapter 4. The description of the people living above the Antonine Wall presented by Cassius Dio, the Roman historian of the Severan period, is as famous for its inaccuracy as for its colour:

The Caledonians and the Maetae dwell among inhospitable hills, between which the land is damp and swampy. The native people have no forts or

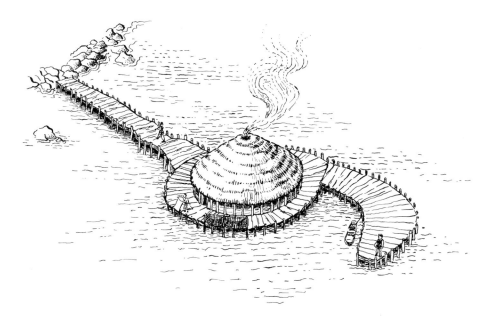

How a loch-house or crannog may have appeared. The causeway linking it to the shore would have been pulled down when the island home was threatened, making the dwelling almost impregnable.

towns, nor do they engage in agriculture; they live rather by tending herds, hunting and plucking berries from the countryside, and though there are teeming rivers and lakes all around, for some reason they do not eat fish. Tents are their only habitation. They wear neither clothes nor shoes, enjoy women in common, raise all their children [not following the practice of infanticide] and have a democratic form of government.

The men of the tribes are warlike, enjoying nothing better than joining a raiding party to seize plunder. Their horses are small but swift and some of the warriors fight from chariots. The infantry, armed with daggers, spears and shields, are remarkably swift moving and tough: they can live for a very long time by eating only bark and roots, and they know the secret of preparing a special food which, if taken in very small quantities, relieves them of all hunger and thirst. When danger threatens they submerge their bodies in the marshes and survive for days with just their heads showing above the surface.

The steep ridge beside Loch Broom, known as Dun Lagaidh, has had an Iron-Age fort, a dun and a castle built upon its level summit. The remains of the stairway which once served the interior of the dun are clearly visible.

Edinshall Broch, fort and hut circles, Borders Region. The presence of a broch this far south has never been satisfactorily explained.

Vivid though this picture may be, it is really a jumble of myth and distorted travellers' tales. It has to be examined with care if we are to learn anything valuable from it.

Writing more than a century earlier, Tacitus believed that the Caledonians were no different from the other Celtic tribes of Britain and Gaul, and archaeological evidence supports this view. A society which could construct a fort as spectacular as Tap o'Noth (Gordon), store its agricultural produce in stone-built souterrains and forge fine pieces of metalwork was far from primitive, even by Roman standards. Furthermore, there is no way that the rich and comparatively well-ordered Pictish civilisation of the Dark Ages could have sprung from barren soil. Dio's stories of semi-naked nomads, therefore, may have originated from those who came into contact with groups dwelling deep in remote Highland glens, whose way of life was very different from that enjoyed by the tribes inhabiting the more fertile eastern areas. His fixation with bogs may have arisen from inaccurate descriptions of crannogs.

Traders and Missionaries

The Roman presence was most strongly felt in southern Scotland, in the region lying between the two walls. But even here, except for the work of Christian missionaries (which is touched on below), external influences on the indigenous culture were slight. There are no secular Roman buildings in Scotland, for example, and there are few signs of native emulation of Roman craft or technology. The only direct evidence of that most obvious Roman export, literacy, comes from a single stone scratched with the first four letters of the alphabet. While there may have been periods of peaceful coexistence between Roman and north Briton, there was clearly less cross-frontier cultural exchange than one might have anticipated. If a few Celts have benefited from economic co-operation with the merchants of Britannia, they saw little reason to adopt other aspects of Roman life. As may be inferred from the speech which Tacitus gave to Calgacus, the British generally viewed the Romans as rapacious predators, intent on subjugation. There was nothing to be gained from trying to work with such dangerous neighbours.

Despite the distrust with which they were viewed, however, from the third century onwards the Romans may have tried to cultivate cordial relations with the tribes immediately north of the wall, rather than control them. The Britons almost certainly had to pay some form of tribute, but they were permitted to keep their supplies of weapons (presumably needed to defend themselves against Pictish marauders). Many hillforts were abandoned, some no doubt at the insistence of the Romans and others because they were considered no longer necessary.

The compromise policy brought tangible benefits to both sides. For their part, the Romans received advance warning of trouble brewing further north, an arrangement which took the strain off the Hadrian's Wall garrison and obviated the need for extensive outposts in a region whose economy found difficulty in coping with any extra burden on its resources. As long as they gave due recognition to their overlords, the Britons inhabiting the broad buffer zone of the Southern Uplands were left to get on with their own lives. From Roman civilisation came the scythe and the iron plough, simple enough implements but significant in their effect on Iron Age agriculture. The presence in the south of a considerable market for British produce and manufactures, and good roads along which to transport them, acted as a stimulus for the Votadini and Selgovae to increase production and strengthen their commercial network. Eight 'loca' – Roman-sanctioned meeting places and trade centres – have been located from the third and fourth centuries. Greater security allowed settlements to spread out from within the protective walls of those hillforts which were still occupied. Lest we imagine too happy a picture, however, it should be remembered that the period of Romano-British concord was largely limited to the third century. Roman finds in southern Scotland from the fourth century are rare, and the hoard of battered Roman silverware buried at Traprain Law in the fifth century was almost certainly plunder – the fruit of conflict, not commerce. Over the Roman period as a whole, hostility was the hallmark of relations between the imperialists and their neighbours.

The people of north Britain did not adopt the pagan gods or rituals of the Classical world, and religious practices of the majority of the region's inhabitants appear to have remained basically the same from the first millennium BC to at least the sixth century AD. Early in the fourth century AD, however, the Emperor Constantine declared Christianity to be the official religion of the empire, after which the new faith was energetically proselytised throughout the area controlled by Rome, and beyond. What this meant for Scotland, we cannot be sure. It would certainly be strange if a few missionaries had not attempted to spread the gospel among the Votadini and southern Picts. But the evidence of

Christianity among these peoples (such as east-west orientated graves and assumptions about the lack of need to send missionaries to southern Scotland) all comes from a later period, so we have no way of telling whether early evangelists had any success in the region immediately above the wall.

Further west we are on safer ground. St Ninian is the first British missionary known to us by name. Having undergone some form of training in Rome, in about 400 he was invited to become bishop of Whithorn (Galloway), from where he launched a mission among the southern Picts. The implication of this is that when Ninian arrived in the south-west he found a Christian community already in existence. He showed his co-religionists how to build a stone church (which Bede tell us was an unusual type of building for Scotland at that time) but apparently he did not feel it necessary to offer them further instruction in the faith. Unfortunately, we do not know whether he was a member of the Romano-British church or, as some scholars believe, he was an early advocate of monasticism. Excavations undertaken at Whithorn during the summer of 1990 produced interesting new evidence which may be able to throw some light on the subject.

It is possible that the pre-Ninian Christian community at Whithorn was established much earlier than had been thought previously. It may have been founded not from Rome but by missionaries from the early Christian churches of the Near East. Ninian apparently did not try to change the practices he found in Galloway and this would link him to the monasticism of the Near East. If all this seems rather far-fetched, it is worth pointing out that British communities on the Atlantic, which stood at the end of a busy trade route linking them to Ireland, Gaul and the Mediterranean, had for centuries looked south rather than east. Whatever the precise nature of the church at Whithorn, the undoubted existence of Christianity in southern Scotland before the Roman withdrawal must surely have meant the presence of some sort of trained priesthood within an ecclesiastical structure. This in turn implies books and learning. Yet again we find ourselves surprised at the variety and richness of Scottish Celtic civilisation.

The Northern Offensive

During the comparatively peaceful period following Caracella's withdrawal of Roman troops from the land of the Caledonians, and while Scotland's first Christian community was taking root at Whithorn, undefended villages spread over the south of the country. Modifications were made to Hadrian's Wall, too. The vallum was allowed to fall into disrepair and rural settlements encroached right up to the rear of the wall itself. Immediately to its north a number of small forts provided defence in depth, while further afield units of irregulars known as *exploratores* operated fact-finding patrols. What was happening among the northern tribes all this while, we do not know. But they were certainly not drawn into regarding the Romans with anything less than bitter hatred. Judging from the evidence of the British attack in 296, the gradual amalgamation of tribes (which had been taking place in the region since the first appearance of the Romans) had continued to the point where it is possible to discern a large Pictish kingdom emerging above the Forth-Clyde line.

The assault of 296 was occasioned by a withdrawal of Roman forces south to fight for the ambitious Allectus against the imperial government. When news of what was happening spread beyond the wall, the northern tribes hastily assembled their forces and harried deep into the undefended imperial province, reaching the great stronghold at Chester. The offensive was undertaken with unusual vigour. Furthermore, it was not conducted solely by Picts. Alongside them was a new people, one which in the future was to play a crucial role in shaping the history of northern Britain: the Scots.

The Roman counter-attack was led by the Emperor Constantius. He was accompanied by his son Constantine who, after his father's death in 306, was declared emperor by the army at York. The imperial recovery followed a pattern that was by now becoming familiar: the wall and attendant forts were rebuilt and a punitive column, accompanied by its fleet, penetrated far above the Firth of Forth to impose strict terms on the Picts. There is some suggestion that the expedition met with more organised resistance than its predecessors. If true, this would support the notion of a waxing Pictish kingdom. Two other innovations in the Roman defences were introduced. Forts were built along the shore to counter seaborne attacks, and the force of *exploratores* was replaced by more flexible *areani*. These were scouts or secret agents, charged with reporting all suspicious or dangerous developments above the frontier. Under the new arrangements there was a temporary return to the calmer conditions which had prevailed during much of the preceding century.

In 342 the northerners attacked again, destroying all forts above the wall and drawing the Emperor Constans across the Channel to deal personally with the situation. At about this time the Atecotti appear, ruthless raiders of the west coast

The massive lintel above the doorway of Dun Dornadilla was needed to support the weight of the drystone walling above. The opening was once much taller than it is today.

of England who were based somewhere in Ireland or north-west Scotland. They were particularly to be feared, ran contemporary rumour, on account of their penchant for cannibalism. From this time cross-border attacks become ever more frequent and serious. We know next to nothing about the relationships between the different groups who participated in the attacks: it would be interesting, for example, to know what part was played by the Votadini and how they viewed the Picts. Were the men from the Grampians seen as liberators, or was their interference in southern affairs resented on account of the dislocation it engendered? All we can safely suggest is that the Votadini and Selgovae, in close contact with their Roman overlords since the first century, certainly developed a greater appreciation of Roman ways than the Picts. As a consequence, after the imperial armies had finally withdrawn, a few vestiges of Roman culture lingered awhile in southern Scotland. The presence of Roman names among the earliest figures in the king lists of the tribes of lowland Scotland is difficult to interpret. A pseudo-Roman name may have been thought to carry greater authority than a Celtic one. Another suggestion is that the rulers of the southern kingdoms of the fifth century traced their origins back to Roman prefects who had been set in authority over them shortly before the Roman withdrawal.

The fragile peace of the frontier lands was broken in 360 and again in 367. The second of these wars witnessed a remarkable example of inter-tribal co-operation, known as the 'Barbarian Conspiracy'. Noting civil disturbance within the empire, the Picts (distinguished as two groups, the *Dicalydonae* and the *Venturiones*), the Atecotti, and the Scots launched a concerted attack on Roman Britain. At the same time the Saxons and Franks moved against northern Gaul. Details of the negotiations which preceded this unique event are not known, but the ability to gather information about the state of the Roman defences, pass it on to potential allies and then organise a simultaneous attack tells us a good deal about the political sophistication of those involved. It also suggests the presence of an accomplished leader who commanded widespread respect. Part of the reason for the conspiracy's success was the complicity of the *areani*, who, bribed by promises of substantial booty, appear to have acted as double agents. They were removed once law and order had been restored.

The central planning of the barbarians broke down soon after the attack had been launched, and once over the border the raiders divided into small bands of booty-hunters. Though the destruction they wrought was very serious, they were unable to regroup when Roman troops began the bloody task of hunting

Burnswark Hill, Annandale, a lofty summit enclosed by a huge Selgovae hillfort in pre-Christian times. Later it was chosen as the site for Roman camps, one of which may have served an an artillery training centre.

A view from Hadrian's Wall into the territory once inhabited by the Selgovae. Roman culture made remarkably little headway among the peoples of northern Britain, and when the wall was abandoned towards the end of the fourth century it soon lost all significance as a frontier.

Strathearn, seen here from the slopes of Dundurn, was a key route between the western and eastern Picts.

them down. This allowed the Romans to recover their position more easily than might have been imagined. Accounts of the attack also exaggerated its severity in order to emphasise the prowess of Theodosius, the commander who by 370 had managed to bring the province back under control.

The great assault of 367 is particularly significant in the history of Scotland, for thereafter the Romans gave up all hope of trying to maintain a presence north of the wall. Instead they recognised the native kingdoms of southern Scotland and relied on them to act as buffers against more aggressive northern tribes. The wall itself was changing, too, developing from a strictly military garrison into something of a ribbon settlement in which farmer–soldiers lived with their families. It was now no longer a dynamic offensive headquarters, but a static, partly civilianised and purely defensive boundary marker.

We do not know when the wall was finally abandoned by Roman soldiers. Indeed, since it had ceased to be a symbol of aggression some time before, from a Scottish point of view the event was largely immaterial. The same can also be said of the withdrawal of the last Roman forces from Britain, and the instruction of 410 that henceforward the province was independent and responsible for managing its own affairs. Though it had not been so formally spelt out, the peoples of Scotland had already been in that situation for a number of years.

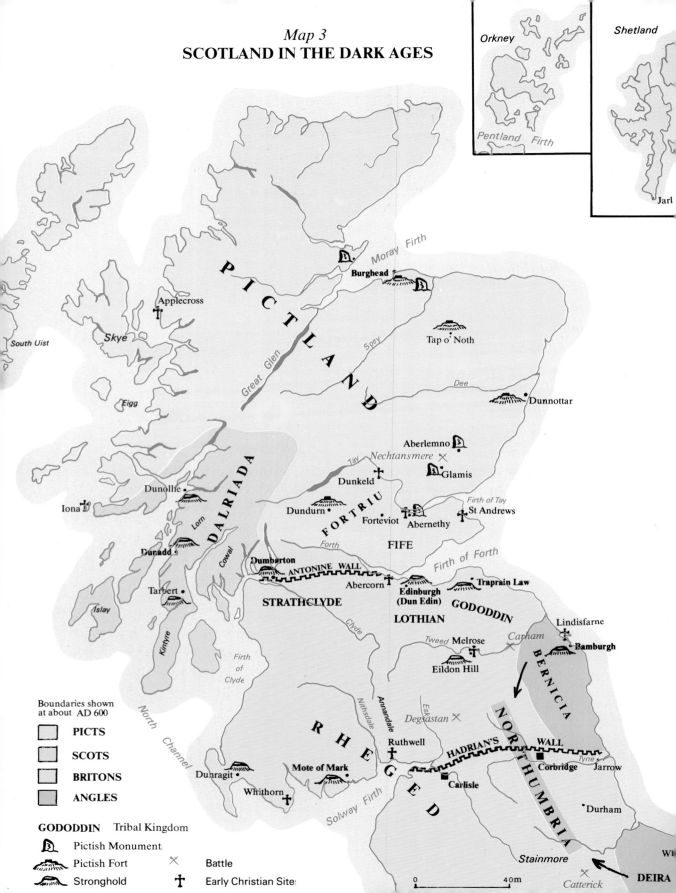

Map 3
SCOTLAND IN THE DARK AGES

Orkney

Shetland

Pentland Firth

Jarl

PICTLAND

Moray Firth

Burghead

Applecross

South Uist

Skye

Eigg

Great Glen

Spey

Tap o' Noth

Dee

Dunnottar

Aberlemno

Nechtansmere ×

Glamis

Tay

Dunkeld

DALRIADA

Dunollie

Lorn

Iona

FORTRIU

Dundurn

Forteviot
Abernethy

St Andrews

Firth of Tay

FIFE

Dunadd

Cowal

Forth

Tarbert

Islay

Kintyre

Dumbarton

ANTONINE WALL

Abercorn

Edinburgh
(Dun Edin)

Traprain Law

STRATHCLYDE

LOTHIAN

GODODDIN

Firth of Forth

Clyde

Lindisfarne

Tweed Melrose

Carham ×

Bamburgh

Eildon Hill

BERNICIA

Firth of Clyde

North Channel

Boundaries shown
at about AD 600

PICTS

SCOTS

BRITONS

ANGLES

R H E G E D

Nithsdale

Annandale

Esk

Degsastan ×

NORTHUMBRIA

Ruthwell

WALL

HADRIAN'S WALL

Corbridge

Tyne

Jarrow

Dunragit

Mote of Mark

Carlisle

Whithorn

Durham

Solway Firth

Stainmore

GODODDIN   Tribal Kingdom

Pictish Monument

Pictish Fort   × Battle

Stronghold   ✝ Early Christian Site

0   40m

Catterick ×

DEIRA

7

THE QUADRIGA I: THE PICTS

The Dark Ages

THE INSUBSTANTIALITY of Roman influence on northern Britain is borne out by the speed with which it evaporated once imperial forces had been withdrawn. The once-mighty forts, already devastated by British assault or deliberately put out of commission by withdrawing Roman soldiers, soon became little more than grassy undulations. Before long the network of Roman roads, though too useful to be ignored completely, had deteriorated into overgrown tracks, distinguishable from traditional pathways only by their directness and the firmness of their surfaces. The massive earthworks of the Antonine Wall were still a significant landmark. But with its timber forts falling into decay and the ditch filling with silt, the wall rapidly lost all military significance. By as early as the mid-sixth century it had become such an obscure monument that Gildas, wholly unaware of its true origins, claimed that it had been constructed by the British (with Roman technical assistance) as a barrier against Pictish incursions.

Gildas made the same claim for Hadrian's Wall. Owing to its fine stone construction, however, this barrier may have provided domestic accommodation well into the fifth century – there was little point in ignoring its substantial buildings just because they carried overtones of a subservient past. Nevertheless, in time even Hadrian's Wall was abandoned. The wooden buildings collapsed and stones were pillaged for other construction. Within a century or so, the physcial remains of the Roman presence served only as poignant reminders of the depressing mutability of human endeavour.

Roman influence on the political, economic and social life of Scotland, never great even at the height of Roman power, disappeared even more rapidly than the empire's physical remains. In the south of the country coinage went out of use by the middle of the fifth century. Archaeological evidence suggests that general commercial activity fell away steadily from the third century onwards, though the discovery in western Scotland of sub-Roman pottery (dating from the centuries immediately following the collapse of the empire in the west) from southern Europe indicates that trade between the Mediterranean and the Celtic north was likely to have been only temporarily severed, if at all.

The amity and amalgamation which the Roman threat had from time to time occasioned between the various Scottish tribes now collapsed entirely. It was replaced by years of somewhat tedious strife between the tribal kingdoms which emerged during the fifth and sixth centuries. As already noted, for prestige purposes some sub-Roman leaders adopted Roman names, but as far as we can tell this was the nearest they came to emulating the sophisticated civilisation which their ancestors had displaced. The only significant legacy to survive into the fifth century was a smattering of Christianity in the south of the country. But even this was not directly attributable to Roman policy: the new religion had been only one of a number of faiths granted official imperial approval, and the Whithorn community probably lay outside the Roman Catholic church. By the seventh century the faith of the Scots was a tangle of paganism and Christianity, with much confused interpolation of the two.

It is unfortunate that the period following the withdrawal of the Roman legions from Britain has come to be known as the Dark Ages. The phrase implies that we have almost no information about what was going on, and that what little we do know makes fairly unpleasant reading. In fact, apart from the evidence illuminated by random beams of classical scholarship, we have more information about post-Roman Scotland – particularly north of the Forth-Clyde line – than about any previous era. Archaeological, linguistic and even written evidence exists in comparative plenty. We have, for example, lists of kings with dates of their reigns – something without parallel for Roman or pre-Roman Scotland. The problem is that many written sources, based on memory, legend and folk tale, are highly confused (as we saw in the case of Gildas' explanation of the Roman walls) and often contradict each other. Furthermore, they are frequently at odds with evidence from other sources. (Those wishing for an introduction to the nature and scale of the difficulties involved in interpreting written Dark-Age sources might like to look at John Bannerman's remarkable *Studies in the History of Dalriada*, a scrupulously scholarly attempt to come to terms with a bewildering document known as 'Senchus Fer nAlban', but hardly bedtime reading.) As a result, from the point of view of information available, we are not dealing with the Dark Ages so much as the Abstruse Ages.

The idea that the period saw civilised society overwhelmed by barbaric hoards – another aspect of its 'darkness' – comes, understandably, from classical sources and is echoed by Gildas, whose *De Excido Britonum* ('The Destruction of Britain') explains the tribulations suffered by the British in the fifth and sixth centuries in terms of divine retribution on a wicked people. A similar theme is taken up two centuries later by the Anglo-Saxon monk Bede. Owing to the accuracy of much that Bede wrote and the power of his language, it has been easy to take the author's wails at face value:

> When they realised that the Romans had gone for good, the Picts and Scots went on the attack. Their assaults were more daring than they had ever been before, and it was not long before they had occupied the whole country as far south as the wall. Here the miserable British garrison went in constant fear for their lives, for the tribesmen used hooks to grapple their enemy and pull them from the ramparts onto the ground below. In the end the British gave up. Abandoning their towns and fortifications, they fled into the countryside where they were pursued and torn to pieces like lambs in the jaws of wild beasts. This forced the homeless Britons to resort to the same tactics as their enemies, robbing and looting to get hold of food. Such behaviour only made the situation worse, and before long all agriculture had collapsed and the population was reduced to keeping itself alive by hunting.

Plausible through this may sound, with its fascinating detail of how the people from the north hauled their opponents from the parapet of Hadrian's Wall and reduced the countryside to desolation, it is clear from what we have already seen of Scottish Celtic culture that Bede presents a distorted picture of events and of the people caught up in them. There was no simple division between barbaric northerners and more civilised people to the south, and the political history of the post-Roman period contains no straightforward tale of Rome's old enemies plunging over the wall to seize what they could now that the overlord had left. What happened was vastly more complicated than that. As well as having to deal with each other, the disunited people of north Britain were also faced with hostile immigrants from Ireland (the Scots) and north-west Europe (the Angles).

As a result, Dark Age Scotland – merely a geographical expression with no marked frontier – comprised a kaleidoscopic patchwork of competing tribes and kingdoms. Since any attempt at a comprehensive account of how these groups related to each other would soon deteriorate into an unintelligible pleach of date, character and location, it is customary to abandon a strictly chronological approach and examine each of the major groupings in turn.

During the early Dark Ages the people of Scotland consisted of the Britons, who lived mostly south of the Forth-Clyde line, and the Scots and Picts who inhabited the area above it. The Votadini formed the British kingdom of Gododdin. Later this and the Selgovae (who disappear as an identifiable group) were absorbed into the Anglian kingdom of Northumbria. Eventually, early in the eleventh century the old territory of the Votadini was acquired by the medieval kingdom of Scotland. The fate of the British Novantae is harder to disentangle. They were organised into the Kingdom of Rheged. When this fell the region came under Viking, Strathclyde and Northumbrian influence before it too was absorbed into an independent Scotland. The Damnonii formed the basis of Strathclyde, another British kingdom of the Dark Ages which eventually formed part of a united Scotland.

Above Strathclyde the Scots from the Irish kingdom of Dal Riata managed to colonise an area roughly equivalent to Argyll, where they superseded the indigenous Epidii, a Pictish sub-group. Scottish Dal Riata, usually known as Dalriada to distinguish it from its Irish counterpart, eventually became an independent nation and the basis of the united Kingdom of Scotland. A separate Pictland survived until the ninth century, when it was amalgamated with Dalriada to form the Kingdom of Alba. Since it was the Picts who, from the fifth to the ninth centuries, controlled by far the largest part of Scotland, it seems sensible to begin the survey with them.

The Picts

Of all the major tribal groupings within Scotland, it is the Picts who provide the clearest continuity between prehistoric and early medieval times. Yet it is the people about whom we know the least. As we saw in chapter 6, the name 'Picts' was used first by the Romans at the very end of the third century to describe a federation of tribes living above the Antonine Wall. Without doubt, however, the change of nomenclature – from 'Caledonians' and 'Maetae' to 'Picts' – did not mean that new inhabitants had moved into the area. In the division of the Picts into *Dicalydones* (north) and *Venturiones* (south), a refinement first appearing in the middle of the fourth century, it is possible to recognise the older tribal names. The *Venturiones* somehow translated from the Maetae, which had originated as the Venicones of Ptolemeic times. Their territory became the basis of the later Pictish sub-kingdom of Fortriu, the first part of Pictland to be taken by Dalriada.

Classical sources suggest that *Pritani* was the name which people of the Iron Age used to describe themselves. It has obvious links with *Priteni*, the generic term during Roman times for all those living in northern Scotland. The meaning of both words is, roughly 'the picture people', referring to the Celtic Iron Age custom, mentioned by Julius Caesar, of painting or tattooing designs on the skin. This explains the wordplay of the Roman nickname for the northern folk who indulged in this practice: *Picti*, or painted people.

The extent to which the Picts were a Celtic people has been much disputed. Some Pictish customs, as well as aspects of their art and language, harked back to the Bronze Age or beyond. But the culture of the upper echelons of society, the sector about which we know the most, was undoubtably Celtic, as are many tribal names (such as the Caereni) and place names (the River Dee, for example, comes from the Celtic 'Deva'). Thus it is reasonable to suppose that the Picts were an amalgam of peoples, some of whom could trace their origins back over several millennia, dominated by a Celtic aristocracy which had made its way into Scotland from the fifth or sixth century BC onwards.

The political structure of the Picts is another aspect of their society which remains obscure. For much of the time Pictland was divided into two sub-kingdoms, each with its own king. Sometimes the two rulers were of equal status, at others one was clearly the over-king and regarded as ultimate master of the whole Pictish people. This was particularly so after the late seventh century when the northern King Bridei had driven the Northumbrians from the territory above the Forth and made his headquarters in southern Pictland. As well as the principal kings, there were a number of under-kings. They may originally have been the chiefs of some of the smaller tribes which formed the Pictish kingdom, and the territorial bases of some of them, such as the King of Atholl, crop up later as medieval baronies.

Little detail is known of the political history of Pictland from c. 400 to c. 550. If later history is anything to go by, the period was fraught with civil disturbance. In

The well in the Pictish fort at Burghead. So skilfully is it made that for years it was thought to have been of Roman construction.

the absence of any hard and fast law of succession, the death of a king or sub-king invariably ushered in a time of strife between competitors for the vacant title. There was always tension over who, if anyone, should exercise the authority of Pictish over-king. Domestic conflict must have been spiced with friction in both the west and south, where there were indeterminate frontiers with Dalriada, Strathclyde and Gododdin. The Scottish settlers from Dal Riata cannot have extended their hegemony over a large part of western Scotland formerly in Pictish hands without much bloodshed. At the same time the Picts were under pressure from the British tribes of the south east, who in turn were being harrassed by the new Anglian kingdoms expanding northwards. The shift of the Votadini headquarters form Traprain Law to Edinburgh (Dun Edin) can hardly have filled the southern Picts with a sense of joyous Celtic solidarity either.

The reason why the Pictish history of the post-Roman period is comparatively lean (though fuller than for preceding centuries) is a lack of written Pictish sources. Date lists are about as barren as similar tables which used to be found in school history textbooks. Moreover, Pictish royal pedigrees were compiled much later and by outsiders. It is only when Pictish affairs impinge upon those of other peoples, or when the church is involved, that we can draw on fuller accounts to shed a little light on the otherwise murky goings on in north-east Scotland.

The Struggle for the North

The first Pictish king who is more than just a name on a list is Bridei, son of the Welsh king Maelcon. Bridei's power base was among the northern Picts, and from his headquarters (to call it a 'court' would perhaps be deceptive flattery) somewhere near Inverness or beside the Great Glen he seems to have exercised an imprecise and fluctuating authority over regions as remote as the Orkneys in the north and Skye in the west. At some time in the middle of the sixth century, Bridei won a considerable victory over Gabran, the most powerful of the Scots in Dalriada, and for a while there was peace between the two nations. We do not know how far to the west Bridei's control extended. The presence of Dalriada must by now have been an accepted fact – Bede's inference that in the later sixth century the King of Picts gave the island of Iona to Columba as a secure base for his missionary work is probably a misunderstanding, since by then Iona was almost certainly not Bridei's to give.

The appearance of St Columba on the scene at this time is the chief reason why Bridei stands out among his faceless contemporaries. He was the first Pictish over-king recorded as having shown an interest in the Christian religion. The account of his meeting with the Irish Saint is a wonderful fairy tale of magic and monster, and it is wrong to assume that it led to the new faith being adopted by the king or his scattered and superstitious people (see chapter 9). As far as the political history of the Pictish nation was concerned, the importance of Columba's mission was that it opened the door to a wave of Irish/Dalriadic influence: it has been suggested that it was King Conall of Dalriada, Gabran's successor, who had cannily urged Columba to try his luck among the northern Picts. Bridei may have worsted the Scots in battle, but by allowing in their missionaries he was unwittingly undermining the cultural foundations of his people's independence.

Bridei died in 584, probably in a battle with recalcitrant southern Picts (the Venturiones or Maetae?). By this time Conall's successor Aidan was restoring the fortunes of Dalriada and threatening Pictish control over the Orkneys and the south-east. He may even have managed to reach the east coast, thereby driving a wedge between the Picts and the nations to their south. This may have benefited the Picts in the short run, for in southern Scotland the old British kingdoms were being absorbed into the powerful Anglian kingdom of Northumbria, and it was the Northumbrian king Aethelfrith who finally put an end to Aidan's supremacy at the battle of Degsastan (c. 603).

For the first half of the seventh century the curtain of obscurity once more descends over the Pictish kingdom. It cannot have been a happy time for the northerners, subjected to fresh Dalriadic aggression from Aidan's grandson Domnall Brecc (c. 630–c. 643) and continually threatened by the ambitious Northumbrians. Comparatively secure in their mountainous strongholds, however, the Picts were still regarded as a major power, for when King Edwin seized power in Northumbria in 617 it was to the safety of Pictland that the sons of Aethelfrith fled. One of them was to marry a Pictish princess and father a future king of the Picts.

In 658 King Oswiu of Northumbria decided that the time was ripe to extend his kingdom above the line of the Forth. Brushing aside Pictish, British and Scottish resistance, he struck north and took over what must have been a good part of the fertile region of southern Pictland. The Northumbrians managed to hang on to their conquest for the next 30 years, receiving tribute from the Scots and holding a frontier (perhaps along the Tay?) between their subject Pictish territory and the free Picts further north.

The fortunes of the Picts were restored by another Bridei, distinguished from his predecessor by the name of his father, Bili. Bridei son of Bili came to prominence during the disastrous revolt of the southern Picts in 672. Drest, king of the independent Picts, was deposed in that year, either as a consequence of the rebellion's failure or in preparation for the uprising. If the latter was the case, then Bridei's first clash with the Northumbrians did not augur well for the future. Inspired by the northern Picts, the uprising was put down by King Ecgfrith of Northumbria with exemplary ferocity – it is recorded that at one point during the campaign, finding themselves separated from the main body of the Pictish army by two rivers, the Northumbrians made a bridge out of the corpses of those they had already slain and then advanced over it to finish the slaughter. The events of the next few years are not easy to interpret. It seems reasonable to assume that Bridei was wisely strenghtening his hold over the northern Picts by securing Dunnottar and the Orkneys before risking another thrust to the south. His opportunity came in 685, the year after King Ecgfrith had alienated Celtic opinion by sending troops to Ireland in pursuit of nomadic Rheged warbands.

We do not know why Ecgfrith decided to undertake a punitive expedition against the northern Picts – perhaps, like several Roman commanders before him, he was responding to a period of irritating Pictish harassment and had decided to teach the raiders a lesson? Bede assures us that Ecgfrith moved north against the advice of his friends, and of St Cuthbert in particular. Be that as it may, though Ecgfrith's motives may have been the same as those of Agricola and Severus, his tactics clearly were not. He failed to shield his army with a fleet and he did not advance with the calculated precision of the imperialists. Instead, under the impression that the Picts were fleeing before him, he allowed himself to be drawn deeper and deeper into the hills. The reward for his vanity was death.

On 20 May, having chosen their ground carefully, the Picts turned and fought. The Battle of Nechtan's Mere, probably near Forfar in Angus, was Bridei's finest hour. The Northumbrian army was wiped out and their king slain. 'From this time onwards', commented Bede, 'English power began to wane, and the Picts recovered all the land which they had lost . . . '. Although Bridei died in 693, the Picts celebrated another victory over the Northumbrians five years later. This was overshadowed by the Anglian triumph on the field of Manaw in 711, after which the Pictish king Nechton came to an accord with the old enemy which secured his nation's southern frontier for many years. The new friendship was reinforced by Nechton's pragmatic acceptance of Northumbrian advice to alter the Easter observance in the Pictish church from the Celtic to the Roman practice. This was just as well, for Pictland was coming under increasing pressure from the nations to the west and south-west.

It is perhaps important at this stage to mention that talk of kingdoms, campaigns and conquests should not obscure the fact that we are dealing with small bands of fighting men and with wars fought for booty rather than territory. Like all other British kingdoms of the Dark Ages, Pictland was dominated by a warrior aristocracy obsessed with glory and the tangible spoils of victory. A man such as Bridei was not particularly interested in geographical frontiers *per se* but in the wealth they embraced. So when in the next century we find the Picts in conflict with Strathclyde and the Scots of Dalriada, it was not because the various leaders had dreams of extending their kingdoms from coast to coast. Such an idea would appeal only to potentates inspired by a map-orientated strategy. Neighbouring Scottish kingdoms promised to be more ready sources of riches than the larger and more consolidated power of Northumbria.

The latter part of Nechton's reign was marked by a long and bitter struggle for power between the king and three rivals. The first signs of trouble began in 713 and did not end until the victory of King Oengus I over his rival Drest in 729. The details of the fighting between rival sub-kings are hardly relevant here, but the disturbances serve to remind us just how fragile political unity among Picts was and how, in using terms such as 'kingdom' and 'nation', we should avoid thinking in anachronistic terms of patriotism and settled systems of government. Pictish, and indeed all Scottish government in the Dark Ages was extremely personal. Although loosely based around geographical features and given cohesion by tribalism, a kingdom was essentially one man's possession and its fortunes rose and fell with him. From the eighth century onwards the ruling families of Pictland became increasingly dominated by the Scots, and in the ninth century a series of Dalriadic kings ruled simultaneously over Dalriada and Pictland. Thus when Kenneth mac Alpin of Dalriada assumed the leadership of the Picts in about 843, for all political purposes the Pictish 'kingdom' ceased to exist.

Oengus I was the last of the great Pictish kings. Indeed, since he may well have been part-Scottish, the Dalriadic take-over of Pictland was probably already under way by the time of his reign. Once he had made sure of his position at home, he renewed his pact of friendship with the Northumbrians and turned his attention to Dalriada in the west. Fighting first broke out in 731, when Oengus's son Brude made a successful sortie into Dalriada. The seizure of Brude while in sanctuary two years later gave Oengus the excuse he needed to take advantage of Dalriada's internal divisions and launch a massive strike right at the heart of Scottish territory. The Picts managed to break through to the west coast, thereby dividing the kingdom and putting themselves in an excellent position from which to organise an even more devastating campaign in 736. The great stronghold of Dunadd was taken and large areas of the country pillaged. After further expeditions in 741 Dalriada was brought completely under Oengus's control.

There are indications before this that the Northumbrians were not happy with their ally's success, for in 740 King Eadberht of Northumbria had broken his peace with the Picts and engaged in some indecisive cross-border raiding. However, it was not from the Northumbrians that Oengus met his come-uppance, but from the powerful British Kingdom of Strathclyde. The survival of Strathclyde over the previous two and a half centuries was no mere historical accident. The closely-knit nation had played a significant part in the internal affairs of the Picts for some while. It was also well organised and quite capable of dealing with Pictish warbands, as Oengus found to his cost in 750. In that year an army led by his brother Talorgen was soundly defeated in Strathclyde and Talorgen killed. Oengus's response was to reforge his alliance with King Eadberht of Northumbria and organise a joint raid on the Strathclyde capital at Dumbarton in 756. He had chosen a fortress too far, and after some initial successes the raiders' forces were destroyed.

Oengus had fought his final battle. Managing somehow to escape the slaughter, he made his way back to the east where he lived for a further five years. But the rash southern adventure had shattered the myth of his invincibility, and though he retained control over Dalriada until his death, Pictish power was probably already on the wane. There is a possibility that had he not overstretched himself by challenging the British of Strathclyde his remarkable achievements up to that point could have endured. Had they done so, the northern part of Britain might now still be named not Scotland but Pictland.

The splendid Class II Pictish stone which can be seen beside the road at Aberlemno, Tayside. The design of the upper part of the raised cross, which is flanked by a pair of angels, resembles that of contemporary Celtic metalcraft.

A bearded Pictish warrior with sword and shield, carved in low relief on the front of the Class II Pictish stone found in the churchyard of Aberlemno. Some scholars believe that the tableau was created to commemorate the great Pictish victory over the Northumbrians at Nechtansmere in 685.

Pictland

Our brief glimpse at the political history of the Picts from the fifth to the eighth century must leave the somewhat misleading impression that in the Dark Ages the largest Scottish kingdom was preoccupied with war, both civil and foreign. Though this may have been true for the warrior class, there is plenty of evidence to suggest that the great majority of Pictland's estimated half million inhabitants were more concerned with the next harvest than with the next king. Primitive peasant agriculture lay at the heart of the economy, and the small settlements of circular houses and their attendant field systems differed little from those which had been in existence since the early Iron Age. The ceaseless round of sowing and harvest measured out brief, hard lives. Some crannogs and souterrains continued in use. Craftsmen fashioned goods – both commonplace and exotic – from metal, clay and bone, and in every community the task of making garments from hides and fleeces involved endless hours of drudgery.

The language spoken by the Picts has puzzled scholars for years, since not one handwritten sentence survives. There are carved stones on which can be found such conundrums as:

besmeqqnanammovvez

and some headway can be made with place names and references in contemporary works in other tongues. In the end, though, the best that can be said is that there appear to have been two languages in use, representing the separate Celtic and indigenous origins of the Picts themselves. One was a form of Celtic which arrived with settlers in the first millennium BC. The other, in which the majority of inscriptions appear to have been expressed, is a non Indo-European language, in some ways akin to Basque and surviving from the remote past. Some of the problems involved in coming to grips with the Pictish tongue(s) arise from the fact that the older language did not have its own alphabet. Furthermore, the dividing line between the two languages inevitably became blurred in what may have been a bilingual culture. The result, as far as the layman is concerned, is that the language of the Pictish tribes remains as strange today as it was to their non-Pictish contemporaries.

Apart from works of art, the most impressive Pictish remains are the forts in which chieftains and kings established themselves. Many are similar to earlier hillforts, but at Burghead (north-west of Elgin) it is possible to make out the remains of what must have been a truly magnificent Pictish stronghold. Occupying an area of almost three hectares, it was defended by a series of tall ramparts which have now unfortunately all but disappeared beneath the modern village. Today the only feature which suggests the splendour of the original fortress is an unusual well of huge proportions and elaborate construction. Indeed, so well-built is it that for years people thought that it was a relic from Roman times. The precise function of the structure is unclear. It might have been simply the water supply for the fortress, though other suggestions, such as a shrine to a water god, are equally plausible. It may, of course, have been multi-functional, a shrine from which life-giving water was drawn and in which offenders were executed by drowning, a common punishment among the Celts.

Pictish Art

Part of the fascination of the Picts is that though we know little of their customs and traditions, and scarcely more of their political history, many thrilling examples of their creative artistry still survive, making our ignorance of the society which spawned it all the more frustrating. The roots of a distinctive Pictish art trail far back into prehistory, to the mysterious rock carvings of the second millennium BC. By the sixth century AD, native traditions of sculpture had combined with Celtic and classical design to produce a style whose aesthetic charm is one of the highlights of native Scottish culture.

The majority of artefacts produced by Pictish craftsmen were fashioned from materials such as wood and woollen thread which have long since rotted away. Thus their skill can now be appreciated only from objects made of non-corroding metals (silver and gold), enamel and durable stone. However, since these would have been entrusted only to the most respected artists, and employed in the manufacture of objects of the greatest value, what survives is likely to be a very fair example of the finest workmanship.

Pictish art is distinguished by its intricate patterns and vivid, symbolic representations of men and real or imaginary beasts. A confident curvilinearity is the hallmark of the style, finding its most powerful expression in burgeoning tangles of branch-like decoration and, more specifically, in ten massive double-linked silver chains, probably worn as status symbols by men of high rank. Pictish brooches are plentiful, as are buckles and fasteners, armlets, bracelets and other small ornaments, all fashioned from silver or bronze and sometimes enlivened with bright enamelling. Birds, dogs, horned serpents and other beasts spring from their beds of thick tracery. Larger objects are more rare, though finds include mysterious hanging-bowls, buckets, spoons and ceremonial weaponry. All objects, large and small, display the same brilliant combination of subtle colouring, bold overall design, fine woven decoration and bewitching symbolism.

The stone carving of the Picts is just as exciting as their metalwork. Scholars divide Pictish symbol stones into two categories, Class I and Class II. The former are the earlier category and probably first made an appearance among the northern Picts in Moray and the north-east of Scotland at some time during the

Goose and fish designs on a Pictish Class I stone at Easterton. The significance of the attractive symbols is unknown.

A massive Pictish ceremonial chain, worn by men as a badge of distinction. The silver from which such articles were fashioned may have come from looted Roman articles.

Solitary and shrouded in mist rolling in from the North Sea, the great rock of Dunnottar was once an important Pictish fortress. The outcrop is now crowned with a more modern castle.

seventh century, perhaps during the occupation of southern Pictland by the Northumbrians. Class I stones and slabs, of which there are over 100 examples, are either uncut or shaped only very roughly. Incised upon one of their surfaces we find a wide variety of artistic design, some abstract, some figurative, and numbering about 50 shapes in all. Popular patterns include V- and Z-shaped rods (often adorned with what appear to be flower designs), crescents, loops and circles (resembling the much earlier cup-and-ring marks) which look like telephone dials. More easily identifiable are everyday objects, such as combs, hammers and mirrors, and creatures drawn from life, such as deer, dogs, ducks, snakes, fish and sea horses. Then there is a whole range of mythical beasts straight from a child's storybook: dragons, double-headed hounds, rams with beak-like faces, lions with human heads, and a weird animal looking like a bear with a thick elongated tail and scaly projections down its back.

Where does this fantastic array of shape and symbol come from, and what was its purpose? Unique in Britain, it is too widespread and painstakingly executed to have been simply decoration done for its own sake. Some claim that the significance of the symbols went back to prehistoric times, and that the craft was rooted in the ancient tradition of rock art. Popular designs had probably been embroidered, carved in wood or, even more transitory, tattooed on human skin long before they were cut in durable stone. The stones could have been set up beside graves to commemorate the dead, or erected to symbolise an important marriage or treaty. Might they have been boundary stones?

Class I symbols appear singly, or in groups of two, three or four. Since animal heads point to the right and the designs are set one above the other, it may be that they were intended to be 'read' one after the other, from top to bottom. One attractive explanation for individual symbols is that they were representations of tribal names – for example, 'the people of the fish', or 'the wolf folk'. This ties in with some earlier names of tribes, though it still leaves a question mark over the fictitious or allegorical creatures, found mainly in the south. Perhaps they originated when two or more tribes amalgamated through mutual agreement or conquest – the lizard-tailed and scaly bear representing the subjugation of the bear tribe by the men of the lizard? Since we are now a long way from history, however, this is probably the point at which to move on to the more easily understood carvings of Class II stones.

There is a school of thought which holds that Class I and Class II symbol stones were both cut about the same time. It seems more likely, however, that the latter, with their sculpted shape and sophisticated low relief symbols, are a later development. The idea of stone carving may have been borrowed from the Romans, explaining the presence of objects not normally connected with the traditional Pictish way of life. Class II stones are cut on both sides, usually with an elaborate Christian cross dominating one face. The coexistence of Pictish symbols and representations with Christian imagery suggests that the two were not necessarily repugnant to each other (or it may mean that in some parts of Pictland early Christianity was merely a new and not exclusive variety of magic; see chapter 9). Two of the finest examples of Class II stones are to be seen in Angus, one in the churchyard of Aberlemno, the other in the garden of the manse at Glamis. Features of the carving on both stones bear obvious comparison with the Gospel art being practised in Northumbria at about the same time, though it is impossible to expand on the relationship between the two. The front of the Aberlemno stone is largely taken up with a great raised cross, cut with a skein of decoration and set in a twisting swirl of elongated creatures. The reverse, framed by a pair of ferocious serpents, carries the only known representation of a Pictish battle scene beneath an array of more conventional symbols. The cross on the face of the Glamis stone is similar to that described at Aberlemno, but its surround is quite different. There are straightforward symbols, human figures brandishing axes at each other, a centaur, another animal and – most singular of all – a cauldron with two pairs of legs projecting from it. Cannibalism? Death by drowning? The reverse of the slab is less well finished and holds only three incised symbols: a snake, a mirror and a fish. How one would like to know what it all means!

8

THE QUADRIGA II:
BRITONS, ANGLES
AND SCOTS

The Heroic Age

OF THE five major tribal groupings in southern Scotland at the time of the Roman withdrawal from Britain, 400 years later only one remained as an independent kingdom. It is unlikely that the change had been accompanied by large-scale genocide. For the bulk of the native population the changes meant simply a prolonged period of upheaval culminating in the replacement of one set of overlords by another. Nevertheless, by about 800 the political map of the region had been completely redrawn, largely at the expense of the British.

Of the fate of the Selgovae, who lived in the remote and inhospitable area of the Upper Tweed in the centre of the Southern Uplands, little is known. Their name means 'hunters' and they may well have been the direct descendants of the hardy Neolithic and Bronze Age peoples who for thousands of years had inhabited the square of territory bordered by the modern towns of Hawick, Moffat, Biggar and Peebles. For a time the Selgovae may have organised themselves into the Kingdom of Bernaccia, before it submitted to the Angles and was absorbed into their aggressive new kingdom of Bernicia. However, as long as the Selgovae did not unduly provoke the Angles to the east or Rheged in the west, there is no particular reason why their late Iron-Age culture should not have endured in some sort of subordinate relationship with their powerful neighbours, akin to that established with the Romans, at least into the ninth century.

The Kingdom of Rheged was forged out of the Novantae of south-west

Scotland, the Carveti who occupied the area around Carlisle, and part of the large Brigantine tribe of northern Britannia. We do not know how the union was created or how strong it was, but it must have been one of the British success stories of the fifth century. If the evidence of place names is to be believed, then by about 600 the power of Rheged extended across a broad swathe of northern Britain, from Dunragit in Wigtownshire to Rochdale in Lancashire. The Rheged headquarters was at the Mote of Mark, south of Dalbeattie above the Urr estuary.

Crucial to the kingdom's survival as a significant power was control of part of the eastern north-south road, known as Dere Street, along which contact could be maintained with the Gododdin, the British kingdom in the east. The base at Catterick, at the head of the Vale of York, was of vital importance. Here the main road from York and the south divides. The eastern branch leads either to the Newcastle-Berwick route north, or along the inland path up Redesdale and Lauderdale. By bearing left at Catterick (or, in modern parlance, at Scotch Corner, where the A66 leaves the A1) the traveller takes the most northerly of the Pennine crossing-points, over Stainmore to Edenside, Carlisle and thence to the Annandale and Nithsdale gaps through the Southern Uplands. When the Britons lost control of Catterick at the end of sixth century the way was open for Anglian expansion west into Rheged and north to Gododdin.

The Kingdom of Gododdin was based around Lothian, the haunt of the Votadini, whose tribal name is echoed in that of the new nation. As we have seen, at some stage in the fifth century the tribe moved its headquarters from Traprain Law to Edinburgh, which, as well as being a natural fortress of unsurpassed strength, better enabled them to control their territories on either side of the Firth of Forth. At one time the Gododdin kingdom may have stretched north to Stirling (Bede's 'urbs Guidi') in the territory of the Manau, where it had a frontier with the southern Pictish sub-kingdom of Fortriu. In the south Gododdin ran down to the Tweed, where it met with the Selgovae and, later, the Anglian kingdom of Bernicia.

The most successful of the sub-Roman British kingdoms was that which grew up around the Damnonii of the Clyde. Little is known of the Kingdom of Strathclyde, whose headquarters was Dumbarton Rock, ('Fortress of the Britons'), except that it proved remarkably resilient. Its northern frontier, extending from Loch Long to the upper reaches of the Forth, was defended successfully against both Pict and Scot. It withstood Anglian ambitions in the south-east and by the tenth century was extending its hold south into the land once controlled by Rheged.

By the middle of the sixth century the kingdoms of the British were dominated by a nominally Christian aristocracy, who regarded themselves as heroic defenders of the true faith and civilised ways against the ever-growing barbarian threat. Theirs was the culture of the hillfort and hall, in most respects similar to that extending over the whole of Britain from Cumbria (the native British name for the lands of the north-west) to Cornwall. It was a warrior society, perhaps slave-owning, whose peasantry were obliged to maintain a privileged caste of swordsmen through hospitality and annual payments in kind. Wealth and status were measured in cattle and moveable valuables rather than land. As in the northern part of the country, wars were fought not to extend frontiers but to seize booty – conquered territory was occupied only to ensure that its inhabitants paid their new masters what was due to them. In the scattered hamlets of southern Scotland, with the exception of the introduction of Christianity, life continued much as it had done since the beginning of the millennium.

The enduring image of the sub-Roman British aristocracy, so vividly portrayed in the poems 'Beowulf' and 'Gododdin', is of strong-armed warriors feasting in their lord's hall. They are wrapped in thick woollen cloaks fastened with gaudy brooches of deep significance, and listen intently to tales of great deeds of impossible bravery, physical strength, valour and steadfast loyalty. To break one's word or flee from the enemy was the ultimate shame – when a coalition of Britons under King Mynyddog of Gododdin was slaughtered by the Northumbrians at Catterick in 600, only one soldier survived the battle.

The values if not the actual events of the period are preserved in the tales of King Arthur. Who the man was who gave rise to the legends we shall never know, but there is a good chance that Arthur was a northern British king living about 500. His memory endures in Arthur's Seat, the peak which looms over the city of Edinburgh, and in the Rheged headquarters on the Mote of Mark: it was for his uncle King Mark of Dumnonia (Cornwall) that Tristan set out on his tragic mission to win the beautiful Isolde. Finds from the Mote throw a surprising light on the degree of sophistication enjoyed in the Rheged court. Apart from the expected brooches, articles of jewellery and implements used by metalworkers, there were pieces of decorated glass which may have originated in the Rhineland and pottery from the Bordeaux region of France. Warlike though the society may have been, it was also quite cultured.

The celebrated Hunterston brooch, an outstanding example of later Celtic art. The names of two Vikings are scratched on the back.

The Angles

The Mote of Mark was destroyed at some time during the seventh century when the massive timber-laced drystone walls were fired, causing the surrounding stonework to become vitrified. Though we cannot be certain who was responsible for this destruction, it is likely that it was the Northumbrians, the most vigorous of the peoples living in southern Scotland in the post-Roman era.

The Angles were a Germanic people whose raids on north-east Britain began during the period of Roman occupation. In the late fourth and early fifth century, the hard-pressed officers responsible for defending the Saxon Shore (Gildas makes a single 'proud tyrant' – Vortigern? – responsible) decided to set a thief to catch a thief, and charged a group of Anglian mercenaries based in the Yorkshire Wolds with the specific task of patrolling the coast and driving off marauders. Needless to say, the tactic rebounded on its instigators, and before long a powerful Anglian enclave had been established, developing later into the Kingdom of Deira. But the Angles did not have it all their own way, at one time suffering a crushing defeat at the hands of the Romano-British hero Ambrosius Aurelianus.

The site of the battle of *Mons Badonicus*, fought at the end of the fifth century, remains a mystery. It must have set back the Anglo-Saxon advance by many years, for later some of the invaders are reported to have returned to the Continent. Yet the Anglian kingdom of Deira survived. In the middle of the next century its name, together with those of its king, Aelle, and the Anglian people, provided an anonymous monk from Whitby with material for a famous series of puns in his *Life of Gregory*: the fair-haired strangers whom the pope encountered in Rome were not Angles, but angels; King Aelle contained the start of a hearty Alleluia!; and Deira was a clear sign that his kingdom was to flee from the wrath ('de ira') of God to the Christian faith.

In the mid-sixth century, traditionally in 547, a chieftain by the name of Ida established the rival Anglian settlement of Bernicia. Based upon Bamburgh, north of Deira, for many years it was little more than a colony of piratical raiders. But gradually it extended its hold over the surrounding countryside, swallowing up the sub-Roman civilisation of Tweeddale with its base at the Trimontium hillfort. It is important to point out here that both Deira and Bernicia were British names, and that Northumbria, the name of the kingdom eventually formed when the two combined, was a geographical rather than a racial expression. There are few place names of Anglo-Saxon origin north of the Tees. The implication is that Northumbrians were not so much a single people as a nation of different races united under a single king.

The presence of two expanding Anglian kingdoms, and the possibility that they might one day unite, caused considerable consternation among the surviving British kingdoms of southern Scotland and at times drew them into unexpected but ultimately unsuccessful defensive coalitions. The situation came to a head towards the close of the sixth century. King Urien of Rheged (c. 570–590) launched a number of campaigns against two of Ida's Bernician successors, Theodric (c. 572–579) and Hussa (c. 585–592), in which he strove to maintain a barrier between the Northumbrian kingdoms by clinging on to the crucial Catterick junction. On one of these expeditions, a villain by the name of Morcant betrayed the king to the enemy and he was slain near Lindisfarne in about 590. The event may be taken to mark the beginning of a slow but inexorable decline in Rheged's power.

Ten years later the Northumbrian gauntlet was taken up by the men of

Gododdin, who headed a large British force attempting once more to drive the Angles from Catterick. Their target was Deira, at that time probably by far the more powerful of the two Anglian kingdoms. It has never been fully explained why Urien should have concentrated his forces against Bernicia, while Gododdin ignored its neighbour and struck at the southern kingdom, based in Yorkshire. The immediate outcome of the Battle of Catraeth, generally assumed to have been Catterick, has already been noticed. Its long-term consequences were of even greater import, for it was the last occasion on which the Britons of southern Scotland made common cause with fellow Britons in Yorkshire, Lancashire and North Wales. From now on the men of the north were on their own, a fact which was to have immense significance in the eventual formation of a separate Scottish kingdom. The battle also prepared the ground for the exploits of the first of the great Northumbrian kings, Aethelfrith of Bernicia (c. 593–c. 617).

It was not only the Northumbrians who followed with interest the exploits of the British expeditionary force of the year 600. During the last quarter of the sixth century, King Aedan mac Gabran of Dalriada had been steadily extending his influence through a number of successful campaigns against his northern neighbours, and it is likely that he took advantage of the discomfiture of Rheged, Strathclyde and Gododdin to drive south-east. This move brought him face to face with Aethelfrith's Bernicians, who were similarly following up the outcome of Catterick by moving into British territory. Bede claimed that Aethelfrith 'ravaged the British more ferociously than any other English king, so that, had he been of the true faith, he might have been compared to King Saul of Israel.' In 603 the men of Bernicia and Dalriada met in Liddesdale at an unidentified place known as Degsastan. The ensuing battle, fought between the peoples who had formed the backbone of the barbarian assault on Britannia some 235 years previously, was one of the most important of the period. Aedan's forces were utterly destroyed. 'From that day until this', wrote Bede 128 years later, 'no Scottish king has dared attack the English in northern Britain.' The way was now clear for the Northumbrians to extend their sway over the whole of southern Scotland.

Aethelfrith's next move was not north, however, but south, against the neighbouring kingdom of Deira. In c. 612 he drove out King Edwin, thus uniting the Anglian kingdoms for the first time. Edwin spent part of his exile in Rheged, where he was baptised by Run, a son of King Urien. The act was significant as it presaged the conversion of the Northumbrians. As master of a single

Northumbrian kingdom, in about 615 Aethelfrith then dealt the British a further serious blow when he moved west and defeated another of their coalitions, thereby separating the Britons of Wales and the west from those in Rheged and Strathclyde. Two years later his luck ran out. Backed by the power of East Anglia, Edwin returned to his homeland, slew Aethelfrith and established himself as King of a united Northumbria (c. 617–633). Surviving members of the house of Bernicia took refuge among the Picts and Scots.

Edwin was re-baptised at York in 627. To the delight of Bede, who fails to mention the original conversion, the deed was performed by Paulinus, a bishop of the Roman church. The ceremony served to emphasise the gulf between Northumbrian civilisation and that of the peoples to the north.

We know little about Edwin's relations with the nations to his north. He was a mighty king, however, whose authority extended south into Wessex and west to Wales and the Isle of Man, so it is perhaps reasonable to assume that during his reign there was a steady erosion of Gododdin and Rheged power at the expense of that of the Northumbrians. Elmet, the small British kingdom nestling in the Pennines which had so far managed to cling on to its independence, finally fell.

At the age of 48 Edwin met his end in Hatfield Chase, victim of a combined attack by the pagan King Penda of Mercia and the Christian King Cadwalla of Wales. Northumbria was then devastated by the victors and the union between Deira and Bernicia broken. Anglian fortunes recovered when Oswald of Bernicia, a son of Aethelfrith who had been in exile since 617, returned from the north. Cadwalla was killed at Heavenfield near Hexham, and Northumberland was united once more. As Oswald was related through his mother to the Bernician royal family, his claim to the whole kingdom was widely accepted, ensuring that his reign was free from conflict with rival claimants.

Oswald's reign (c. 633–c. 643) marks an important step in the relations between Northumbria and its neighbouring British kingdoms. After his 16 years of exile among the Picts and Scots, the new king of Northumbria knew his potential enemies well, and it is likely that he drew on the information he had gathered to undermine still further the tottering power of Gododdin and, perhaps, that of Rheged too. In 638, for example, Edinburgh was being besieged. Though we are not told what the outcome of the assault was, it is very likely that the event signified the final extinction of an independent Gododdin, some two centuries after its creation. Had this not been the case, then it is difficult to make sense of Bede's comment that 'under the king's sceptre lay all the provinces and kingdoms of Britain, whether they spoke British, Pictish, Scottish or English.' Obviously such a remark does not imply physical occupation by Northumbrian soldiers, but rather an acceptance of Oswald's overlordship by all lesser potentates.

Just as he had at the end of Edwin's reign, it was Penda of Mercia who engineered the collapse of Northumbrian supremacy, attacking Oswald in about 643 and killing him in battle near Oswestry. Again the Northumbrian kingdom divided in two. Oswiu, who managed to establish himself on the throne of the now independent Bernicia, probably maintained the strong links with Pictland which had been set up during Oswald's reign, for in 654 he fled to Stirling when threatened by yet another Mercian incursion into Northumbrian territory. This was to be the last time that Penda disrupted the Anglians, however, for somehow Oswiu regrouped his forces in the north and slew Penda at Winwaed, near Leeds. With his southern frontier secure and Northumbria reunited, Oswiu now turned his attention to the north. Perhaps during his brief sojourn at Stirling he had noted the weaknesses of the southern Picts, the nation with whom, now that Gododdin was no more, Northumbria had a common frontier. In 658 the Northumbrians swept into southern Pictland carrying all before them and carving out a huge northern province for themselves above the Forth.

We do not know how far Oswiu ventured against the rump of Rheged, but it is reasonable to suppose that he encouraged an Anglian advance to the west as well as to the north. There is more specific evidence of such a policy during the reign of Oswiu's successor, Ecgfrith, who may well have overseen the final eclipse of the kingdom based upon the Mote of Mark. From 682 onwards there are reports of British warrior bands in Ireland. Though we cannot be certain whence they came, it is possible that they were dispossessed groups of Rheged warriors who had been driven overseas before the advance of the Northumbrians along the northern bank of the Solway Firth. This would explain the unusual presence of Northumbrian soldiers in Ireland in 684, the year before the successful Pictish uprising.

The Northumbrians managed to hold down their Pictish province for 30 years, successfully quashing the serious uprising in 672. King Bridei finally drove them from all land above the Forth in 685. Although there was desultory fighting between Pict and Angle along this border for many years to come, the frontier remained essentially the same until the ninth century, when both nations found themselves facing an entirely new and even more dangerous threat: the Vikings.

The rock of Dundurn on which a substantial fort guarded the western frontier of Pictland against incursions from Dalriada.

The gigantic outcrop known as Traprain Law looms over the flat plain of East Lothian like a stranded whale. For many centuries the capital of the Votadini, it was abandoned in favour of Edinburgh by the British kingdom of Gododdin.

The extent to which Northumbrian arms were followed by an Anglianisation of native society and culture is uncertain. The remarkable Ruthwell Cross, completed in about 690 and showing clear signs of Northumbrian influence, is believed to have been erected to indicate the furthest extent of the Anglian advance at the time. Not until 731 do we find a Bishop of Whithorn with an Anglian name – Pehthelm – and the last Anglian bishop left the see less than a century later, in 803. In other words, though the Northumbrian kings may have held political sway over the territory of the former kingdom of Rheged, this was not accompanied by any wholesale acceptance of alien ways by the native population. English place names are not common in Galloway, and to the north the Kingdom of Strathclyde remained largely untouched by Northumbrian ambitions.

The situation in Lothian, the northernmost territory which the Northumbrians held for any length of time, is more complex. Here society seems to have been an amalgam of British and Anglian ways. Native place names, such as Peebles and Melrose, exist alongside Coldingham and Haddington, which are clearly English. An Anglian bishop, Trumwine, was established at Abercorn in 681 but he was forced to flee south after the battle of Nechtansmere (685) and his seat never returned to Northumbrian hands, suggesting that the Lammermuirs rather than the Forth marked the effective limit of lasting Anglian authority.

By the eighth century the situation in Scotland was completely different from that left by the Romans 300 years previously. A multiplicity of tribes and petty kingdoms had been reduced to only four. Of the various British kingdoms, only Strathclyde remained. Much of the territory to its south and east was dominated by the Anglian Kingdom of Northumbria. In the north and east the Pictish nation held sway. Finally, in the north-west there was the hard-pressed Kingdom of Dalriada.

The Scots of Dalriada

Bede might not have been unduly surprised had he been told that one day all the peoples of northern Britain would be united into a single kingdom. After all, since the withdrawal of the Romans there had been a gradual process of amalgamation among the provinces and kingdoms of Britain, and southerners already accepted the concept of the 'Bretwalda', or over-king, whose supreme authority was accepted by all lesser monarchs. However, had he been told the name of the new kingdom, he certainly would have raised a scholarly eyebrow. He might have expected Pictland, or even Northumbria. But Scotland? The very word was alien to him. The only similar one he knew was Scotia, and that referred to Ireland.

The North Channel separating Kintyre from the north-western tip of Ireland is only 12 miles wide. Throughout history there has been a constant coming and going of traders, warriors, missionaries and settlers across this narrow, busy seaway. At some time in the fourth century it witnessed the first of a series of voyages which in the fullness of time was to acquire a greater significance than any other across those unpredictable waters. The vessel, presumed to have been constructed of a wicker frame securely wrapped in well-tallowed hides, rolled uneasily north-east, making for the Mull of Kintyre. It was propelled by oarsmen, though when the wind was favourable a light sail was raised to make their task easier. The crew were Gaelic-speaking Celts of the Scoti (the name means 'bandits') tribe from Ireland seeking a favourable spot in which to establish a settlement in Britain. During the course of the next century or so they were followed by others, some arriving as settlers, others merely as pirates looking for booty in north-west Britain, so that by 500 there was a sprinkling of Scots along the western seaboard of southern Scotland.

The Scottish settlement acquired significance only at the very end of the fifth century (perhaps about 497) when Fergus Mor son of Erc, a man of royal blood from the same stock as St Patrick, who had recently helped convert his people to Christianity, arrived in Argyll with his sons and, perhaps, his brothers to found a colony of the Irish kingdom of Dal Riata. (The indigenous population of the area, a Pictish tribe known as of Epidii, disappear without trace.) The reasons for Fergus's move are unclear, though it probably arose as a result of political pressures owing to rising population and land shortage. It is incorrect to think of the Scottish Dalriada as being a single political unit in the sixth century. It was really just a collection of people, some of whom had preceded Fergus to Scotland and so may have resented his arrival.

The four main groupings in early Dalriada were the *cenel* (tribe or kin-group) of Oengus in Islay, *Cenel Loairn* in Lorn (north of Loch Fyne), and Fergus's descendants the *Cenel Gabrian* and *Cenel Comgaill* in Kintyre and Cowal (south of Loch Fyne). In the tenth century the *Cenel Oengus* (Angus) and *Cenel Loairn* were believed to have been founded by two of Fergus's brothers, Angus and Loarn, but this is unlikely. More probably they were groups of earlier immigrants. Fergus was succeeded by his son Domangart 'of Kintyre', then by Domangart's sons Comgall (died c. 538) and Gabran (died c. 558) from whom the *Cenel Comgaill* and *Cenel Gabrain* were descended.

Political unity among these scattered peoples was provided by general acceptance of the need for an over-king. By the middle of the sixth century this figure is likely to have been provided by the *Cenel Gabrain*, since they were simultaneously kings of Dal Riata. When in about 558 Gabran was killed in battle with Bridei son of Bili, King of the Picts, the overlordship passed to Conall, son of Gabran's predecessor, Comgall. Conall's authority was sufficiently widely accepted in about 563 for him to be able to give Iona, in the *Loairn* territory, to St Columba. It may be that in more settled times such a high-handed act would not have been looked upon so favourably, but now, faced with the real possibility that Dalriada might be wiped off the map by the Picts – the nation from whom, after all, Iona had originally been stolen – the Scots were prepared to accept any measure which helped their resistance. Since they could not afford to fight on two fronts, it was vital for them to maintain good relations with their compatriots in Ireland. Throughout their early history the Scots gained much succour from their strong links with the Christian church. The support of so powerful a figure as Columba could not be declined lightly.

The Pictish assault, and references to Dalriada's contacts with other neighbouring kingdoms, surely mean that the new Scottish settlement had alredy made its power felt in the region. For the Picts to have regarded the Scots as a people worth attacking only about 60 years after Fergus's landing suggests that Dalriada had accumulated wealth and had already started to expand its overlordship to the south and east. Though we have no idea of the numbers involved, it is very likely that, when tales of the colony's early success reached Ireland, fresh boatloads of immigrants sailed to join the pioneers in Argyll.

Early Dalriada was a maritime state. A quick glance at the map will show that its warriors must have been as much sailors, or marines, as soldiers. The kingdom was essentially a federation of islands, peninsulars and narrow coastal strips. The sea was its highway and boats were its war chariots. Its forts, such as the *Gabrain* stronghold at Tarbert or those of the *Loairn* at Dunadd or Dunollie, did not watch over roads or river crossings, but stood guard close to the coast. The aristocracy accepted tribute in the form of oar-service and in 719 we are told that Dalriada's internal conflicts gave rise to a naval battle between rival warlords, something inconceivable to the land-based British or Pictish warriors. Dalriada's strong maritime traditions must have stood her people in good stead in the ninth century, when Britain was threatened by the sea-borne raids of the Vikings.

Apart from the strong maritime influence on their culture, the Scots of Dalriada differed little from the other peoples of Scotland at the time. Theirs was basically the same Celtic warrior society as we have seen in Gododdin, Rheged and Northumbria, in which the task of the bulk of the population was to support the soldier aristocracy. Excavations at Dunadd and other sites reveal traces of a culture not dissimilar to that which flourished to the south on the Mote of Mark. Agriculture, trade and skilled manufacture in metal and other materials were not sacrificed to the needs of war.

Kings and Conquests

The first king of Dalriada to win widespread recognition was Aedan mac Gabran. He came to power in 574, making him a contemporary of Urien of Rheged and Aethelfrith of Bernicia. Aedan's early life is something of a mystery. As a son of the discredited Gabran, he may have fled to the east after his father's death and set up some sort of power base of his own on the Forth. While here he possibly married a Pictish wife, which would explain how his son Gartnait later became King of the Picts. His time in the east also taught him about his potential enemies and no doubt strengthened his resolve one day to live down the humiliation and discomfort of exile. By 574 he had the reputation of a man to look out for, a ruthless soldier and a competent administrator fired by a driving ambition. These qualities had already attracted Columba's attention. The new king established himself in Dalriada by force, and was ordained by Columba. The following year he crossed over to Dal Riata in order to exert his supremacy over the Irish part of his territory.

Over the next 30 years Aedan rushed hither and thither in a series of stormy campaigns which made him one of the most feared of the northern kings. He struck at the Picts on several occasions, defeating them in the region of Stirling but driven back when he ventured further north into the Pictish heartland. His vessels harried the Orkneys and may even have travelled right round the coast to the Forth in search of loot. At least twice he met the forces of King Aethelfrith, the first time in 598 and secondly at the fateful battle of Degsastan, when he was utterly crushed. The defeat may have cost him his throne, for when he died in 608 he was no longer regarded as King of Dalriada.

Aedan's spectacular but piratical career had little lasting effect on Dalriada. It was the story of a super-brigand, not a statesman, and the king's victories were not accompanied by attempts to impose Dalriadic government on the vanquished. As a result, after Aedan's death his kingdom was eclipsed somewhat by the power of Strathclyde. An indication of the strength of this most successful of the northern British kingdoms comes from the reign of Aedan's grandson, Domnall Brecc (c. 630–c. 643). Brecc appears to have tried to emulate his grandfather's exploits, but with little success. He fought in Ireland and, inevitably, against the Picts, on each occasion failing to secure any notable victory. In the end he was killed at the Battle of Strathcarron, overwhelmed by the forces of King Owen of Strathclyde.

British Strathclyde has not caught the popular imagination in the way that the Picts or Scots have done. Nor does it have the romantic appeal of the ill-fated Gododdin or Rheged. Nevertheless, during the seventh and eighth centuries it was in some ways the pivot around which much of Scottish history turned. Picts waxed and waned, the Northumbrians came and went, and the Scots flashed across the northern sky from time to time; but the men of Strathclyde remained constant in their Dumbarton stronghold, defying anyone to dislodge them and exercising extensive control over the vital Forth-Clyde plain and the neighbouring kingdoms. As we have seen, it was the Strathclyde British who humbled Domnall Brecc. Subsequently they seem to have played an important part in the internal affairs of their neighbours in Dalriada.

The Picts were not immune from Strathclyde's influence either: in the seventh century King Neithon of Strathclyde (died c. 621) and his grandsons may well have ruled over the southern Picts as well as their own people. This would make the defeat of Domnall Brecc and the consequent intrusion of Strathclyde into Dalriada even more significant, for it meant that the family of Neithon exercised some form of lordship over most of northern Scotland. It is also possible that the successful Pictish revolt against the Northumbrians in 685 was masterminded from Strathclyde.

The power of Strathclyde endured far into the next century, too. In 752 the might of the all-conquering Pictish king Oengus I broke against the rock of Dumbarton. Not until more than a hundred years later did the strength of an independent Strathclyde finally crack in the face of Scottish expansion and Viking assault. As in the case of the Picts, lack of information prevents a detailed exposition of the crucial part played by Strathclyde during the Dark Ages. But only when allowance is made for this vital bit of the puzzle can the other pieces of the early Scottish jig-saw be fitted into their correct places.

In the later seventh century Dalriada deteriorated into a tangled web of internecine feuding. Sometimes a figure emerged as over-king for a while, as did Ferchar Fota of the *Cenel Loairn* in the 670s, only to fall back into obscurity – in Fota's case owing to the intervention of Strathclyde, for whom the chaos among the Scots must have been most welcome. Part of the problem was that there was no established manner of selecting a new over-king. A monarch was supposed to emerge from the family of his predecessor, a sure recipe for civil war. By about 700 the Scots had devolved into at least seven competing family groups, each headed by their own king. It can be argued that the situation was ripe for a Pictish take-over, as may have happened when King Oengus was proclaimed overlord of Dalriada in 741. In fact, what appears to have been going on was a gradual merger through marriage of the Pictish and Scottish ruling families. We have already seen how as early as the late sixth century a son of Aidan became King of Pictland, and even Oengus I may have been more Scottish than Pictish. The ruling classes of both nations were of Celtic stock and racial distinctions almost certainly meant less to contemporaries than to later chroniclers. During the eighth century several Pictish kings had Scottish blood in their veins. A few generations later the take-over was almost complete, paving the way for Kenneth mac Alpin, King of Scots, to become accepted as King of Picts as well, thus uniting the whole of northern Scotland in the Kingdom of Alba.

9

CHRISTIANS AND PAGANS

A New Faith

ACCORDING TO Bede, once persecution of Christians ceased in fourth-century Roman Britain, their faith:

> spread steadily all over the Province. Well-endowed shrines were built to commemorate the martyrs. Christian festivals were observed and the Church's practices followed with piety and sincerity.

Nevertheless, as far as we can tell, Roman Christianity made as little headway in northern Britain as other aspects of imperial culture. Largely unaffected by the momentous political changes taking place further south, the new faith seems to have seeped slowly north-east from the region of Galloway, entering the British kingdoms of Rheged, Strathclyde and Gododdin during the fifth and sixth centuries. The achievement was managed without striking martyrdoms. It threw up few saints of the premier division and appears to have followed no regular geographical pattern. St Kentigern (c. 520–c. 612), for example, who was summoned by King Riderch Hen of Strathclyde to preach the faith to his subjects, is credited with founding a church at Glasgow. Since Kentigern may have had Votadini blood in his veins and had spent his early life in southern Pictland, the implication is that in Strathclyde he was an easterner working among westerners. The relatively haphazard nature of the early conversion is also suggested by the remark that Kentigern (or Mungo, 'dear friend') came across a Christian cemetery at Glasgow which was reputed to have been in existence since before St Ninian's time. Finally, mention should be made of St Patrick

(c. 389–c. 490?), a British missionary – possibly from Strathclyde – whose work was vital to the spread of Christianity to Ireland and thence, later, to Dalriada.

The outcome of this steady yet piecemeal missionary work was that by the early sixth century the peoples of southern Scotland had adopted their own distinctive Celtic Christian culture. Archaeological evidence, in the form of burials in east-west orientated graves closely resembling much older cists, supports such a hypothesis. Commemorative stones and other evidence suggest that the church had some form of loose episcopal structure, though by the sixth century it was beginning to acquire the monastic predilection for which it is famed. This may have resulted from continuing intercourse along the Atlantic route. In the fourth century St Martin of Tours, who corresponded with St Ninian, had founded his own peculiar monastery in Gaul, and St Ninian dedicated his new stone church at Whithorn to his deceased friend. It is also possible that the ascetic side of Christianity, which flourished in the arid lands of the Near East, may have had a similar appeal to the early Christians dwelling in the troubled and rugged regions of northern Britain.

Before we move to the work of St Columba and the extension of Christian influence to the Picts and Angles, it is worth looking briefly at the significance of the Christian mission and its attraction for the pagans of northern Britain. Although late twentieth-century western society may be regarded as a post-Christian civilisation, it is still permeated by the values and morality of the traditional faith. The ideals of the gospel of love, however feebly adhered to in practice, are taken for granted by the majority of the population: peace is ultimately more worthy than war, riches are no end in themselves and it is the duty of the fortunate to care for the disadvantaged. It is difficult for us to imagine civilisation without such a moral code. Yet only by doing so can we appreciate the impact that the Christian holy men made on pagan Britain. It was not really a question of replacing several gods by one, or of building fine churches, but of offering people new standards, suggesting to them that real strength lay in showing consideration, mercy and love for others. Let one example suffice. In 697 at the Synod of Birr in Ireland, Adomnan, a successor to St Columba as Abbot of Iona, managed to persuade a formidable gathering of leading clerics and secular rulers from all over Ireland and northern Britain to accept his 'Law of Innocents'. The pronouncement's aim was to shield from the horrors of war all those unable to defend themselves, such as children, women, and priests. Massacres and cruelties continued, of course, but Adomnan's guidelines surely mark a significant advance away from the unsympathetic world of Druidic religion.

The Laws of Adomnan were the exception rather than the rule. Christianity would not have been able to take on the pagan world successfully without a good deal of compromise. To the ordinary man and woman it must at first have appeared as just a new and more powerful form of magic. Adomnan's life of Columba and similar early Christian writings are full of stories in which the Christian God proves himself more powerful than His rivals by enabling His saint to perform miraculous tasks, such as overcoming the Loch Ness Monster (fortunately for the future economy of the region, he did not kill it) and controlling the weather. Pagan festivals were adapted to the new calendar. Fresh symbols (at first the Greek *chi-rho*, the initial letters of *Christos*, then the cross) replaced, or were simply given prominence over older signs. Ancient shrines, such as wells and rocks, continued to be venerated. As now, very few believers can have concerned themselves with theological profundities like the Incarnation or Transubstantiation. Yet for all the simplicity and crudity of their beliefs, the Christians of the Dark Ages must have sensed that their new faith held something different. It is true that many adopted a nominal Christianity at the behest of their ruler, and such faith could wither as quickly as it had sprung up. But there were still a substantial number for whom conversion meant a good deal. They were not just members of the privileged elite, nor was their change of faith based solely on fear. Christianity's strength lay in the breadth of its appeal. Here was a religion for everyone, including groups hitherto largely ignored by the priesthood: women, slaves, the poor and the disadvantaged.

Christianity had a marked impact on the culture of north Britain. It was the vehicle by which a tradition of learning was first introduced into the region and then sustained through to medieval times. Each tranquil monastery was multi-functional, serving as church, school and art centre. Roughly rectangular in shape and defined by a low wall and ditch, the monasteries generally comprised one or two larger buildings which were surrounded, in keeping with the root of the word 'monastery' (meaning a solitary living place), by tiny individual cells, each with its cold stone bed. The communities, some of which sheltered at least 20 inmates, were made up of single people of the same sex who had renounced worldly comfort and chosen to follow a measured life of prayer, work, contemplation and scholarship. Dressed in simple cowls, white tunics of coarse cloth and leather sandals, they supported themselves by subsistence farming. Fully

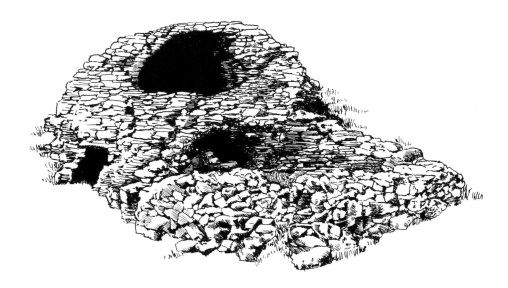

The tumbled remains of a Celtic monastic cell in which a monk slept, meditated and prayed in solitary tranquillity.

fledged monks were known as 'seniores', novices (student brothers) as 'juniores', while 'working brothers' looked after the animals, undertook building work and laboured in the fields. Following the example of Columba at Iona, the abbot was spiritual father and governor of the whole enterprise. Each monastery was an attempt to recapture an ideal, a little haven of ascetic tranquillity founded upon prayer and meditation of life's infinite mysteries. And here, in the care of respected men whose horizons stretched beyond the activities of local war bands or the state of the harvest, were found precious manuscript books and articles of rare beauty – glimpses of a less cruel and sordid world.

Columba and the Picts

The man most closely associated with the development of Christianity in Scotland is St Columba (521–597), a member of an Irish royal family who may not have set foot on Scottish soil until the age of 42. His life previous to this is conveniently passed over by his biographer Adomnan, probably because it did not accord with the hagiographic image of pacific holiness which he wished to portray. Humility does not appear to have been one of Columba's more pronounced characteristics and, unlike St Francis and others whose admission of early sinfulness served to emphasise later virtuosity, he does not appear to have acknowledged that the years before his mid-life crisis were anything other than wise preparation for a Highland mission.

Columba was a strong and vigorous individual. Not many of his contemporaries survived into their forties; precious few of those who did would have been up to crossing the open sea in a 13 seater coracle and then setting out on an exhausting second career, involving extensive travel through inhospitable terrain and all manner of physical danger. While judiciously avoiding too definite a conclusion, Alfred Smyth has suggested that, although a priest, Columba found it most difficult to put behind him the warrior traditions of his class and upbringing. All his life he took an interest in things military and political, asking after the result of a battle as we might seek to know the final score in a football match. An unwise decision to fight beside his kindred in the battle of Cul Drebrene (561) may explain both the large scar on Columba's side (Adomnan said it was the result of an argument with an angel) and his subsequent excommunication.

The terms of Columba's pardon, issued at Teltown a while later, may have included a period of penance (or even permanent exile) among the Scots of Dalriada. Whatever the reason for his leaving Ireland, in 563 Columba arrived in Scotland with twelve companions, intent on putting his past behind him and doing God's work to the best of his considerable ability. The number of friends said to have accompanied him is significant, and by no means the only parallel drawn by Adomnan between Columba and the One in whose footsteps he followed: the Irishman too turned water into wine and raised the dead.

During his 34-year mission in Scotland, Columba established a formidable reputation. Much of this was due to the aura of saintliness which grew up around him. It also rested on his undoubted administrative ability, his energy and the confidence which came easily to one from a royal background. His chief contributions to the fledgling Scottish church were the prestige which he brought to the institution, and the support he gave to the monastic movement, particularly by the foundation of the Iona community, 'the most important of almost all the monasteries of the northern Scots and Picts' (Bede). To Bede's surprise Columba subordinated the secular to the regular clergy:

St Oran's Chapel, Iona, the oldest surviving ecclesiastical building on the island.

Iona is always ruled over by an abbot, who has power not only over his own community but over the whole of the surrounding province as well, even its bishops. This tradition began with the founder of the community, who was not a bishop but a monk.

Columba did not convert the Scots of Dalriada, for by the time of his arrival it is likely that the new faith was already quite soundly established among them. His missionary work among the Picts, if that really was the purpose of his northerly perambulations, was of doubtful durability. Under Columba and his successors (who were drawn from his kin) Iona became one of foremost monastic centres of western Europe. It was not merely a stepping stone between Ireland and Scotland – Columba may not have set up his monastery there until ten years after his arrival – but an outstanding international centre for Christian thinking and art. From Iona the monastic movement spread north. During Columba's lifetime, religious houses were established at Durrow, Hinba and several other sites.

Writing about a century after his subject's death, Adomnan has a fine story of the first meeting between Columba and Bridei, King of the Picts:

When the Saint made his first difficult journey to see Brudei, the proud and arrogant king refused to open his castle gates to the new arrival. On seeing this, Columba went up to the gates, made the sign of the cross upon them and knocked. At once the bolts drew back of their own accord and the gates flew open, whereupon Columba and his companions walked into the castle unhindered. Dumbstruck, Brudei and his court immediately ran out and greeted their visitors with suitable reverence and pacifying words. From this time forward Brudei held Columba in very high esteem.

By Bede's time the exploit had become distorted to: 'by preaching and example Columba converted the Picts to Christianity'. In fact Columba did nothing of the sort. He certainly met Brudei on several occasions, struck up some sort of relationship with him and had a few hair-raising tussles with the king's Pictish magicians. But for all his supernatural wizardry, Columba did not succeed in persuading the Picts to join his church. It is unlikely that a single monastery was founded in Pictland during his lifetime.

The conversion of the Picts, the last of the Dark Age peoples of Scotland to accept Christianity, was a long and slow process. In northern areas pagan burial customs remained in fashion until the eighth century. There is no evidence of a seventh-century Pictish scriptorium (a place where manuscripts were written) and Class II Pictish stones with Christian markings almost certainly date from the eighth century. In the south, early missionary work may have been undertaken by men from Rheged and Gododdin, and later by Northumbrians, though initially the influence of the latter did not reach above the Tay. Christianity was introduced to the upper parts of the kingdom during the later seventh and early eighth centuries by missionaries from Dalriada. This lends credence to the view that though the political fortunes of the Scottish kingdom may have waned from the first half of the seventh century onwards, its cultural influence did not.

The first serious work in the north-west was undertaken by Donan, a little-known Celtic saint. Working independently of Columba, he travelled around the Hebrides and the western seaboard (where he is remembered in the name of Eilean Donan in Loch Duich) until martyred on Eigg in 617. His mission was resumed later in the century by St Maelrubbha (died 722) who in 673 founded a monastery at remote Applecross in Wester Ross, overlooking Raasay and the grey peaks of Skye. Few now remember the pioneering labours of Donan and Maelrubbha. They were not as well connected as Columba or his followers, and no doting disciple wrote up their lives. But their low-key missions among the hostile Picts were crucial in spreading the new faith to the more isolated corners of the land. As a result of their efforts, and those of numerous other unsung missionaries, we may assume that by about 750 all the territory of present-day Scotland was nominally Christian.

Northumbria and the Influence of Rome

The Anglian invaders who settled north of the Humber had minimal contact with Christianity before their arrival in Britain. Indeed, as we have seen, they were regarded by some as pagan barbarians set by God as a punishment for the backsliding of the faithful. However, given the proximity of their settlements in the north of Britain to the Christian British kingdoms of Elmet, Rheged and Gododdin, and the zeal of the Christian community in carrying their message to the unbelievers, it was not long before Deira and Bernicia found themselves under pressure to join the Christian fold.

The situation was complicated by the presence of a second missionary front, approaching from the south. According to legend it was the sight of pagan

Old Wick Castle (12th century), a stark reminder of Norse power in the north and west of Scotland.

The road along Strathearn from Dalriada to Pictland, a route which may have been taken by Kenneth mac Alpin when he expanded his authority to the east in about 742.

Anglians in Rome which inspired Pope Gregory to send St Augustine on his mission of 597 to convert the English. The teachings and practices of Rome were not exactly the same as those of the ancient Celtic church in the north. There were differences over the method of computing the date of Easter, the relative authority of bishops and abbots, the consecration of bishops, baptismal rites and a number of comparatively minor matters such as the correct style of tonsure. Thus the Northumbrians found themselves evangelised by two Christian groups who did not see eye to eye. The decision as to which set of practices to adopt often depended not on theology but on politics.

While in exile among the Britons c. 612–c. 617, in what may have been a genuine change of faith or merely a polite way of repaying hospitality, King Edwin of Deira was converted to Christianity by teachers of the Celtic church. When Edwin returned as king of a united Northumbria, therefore, the way was open for Christian influence to flood in upon his people. The early Northumbrian church was thus established according to the northern rules. The situation was complicated by the arrival from the south in about 627 of Paulinus, an experienced Roman missionary who had appeared in Britain in 601 as part of Augustine's much-needed reinforcements.

Edwin now had to decide between the version of the church into which he had already been admitted, and that promoted by Rome. As Bede makes clear, the difficulty was resolved not by hours of prayer but by political expediency:

> Edwin sent an embassy south to request the hand of Ethelberga of Kent in marriage. He was told, however, that a Christian maiden was not allowed to marry a heathen husband . . . . When Edwin heard this reply he made a number of undertakings: firstly, he agreed to tolerate Christianity within Northumbria; secondly, he undertook to allow Ethelberga and all her entourage full freedom of worship; thirdly he promised to become a Christian himself if his court agreed.

In other words, Edwin ditched the Celtic church in favour of the Roman as the latter brought with it the prospect of an important alliance with one of the most powerful of the English kingdoms. He was re-baptised in 627, and Paulinus was rewarded by being made the first Archbishop of York. As a result of this volte-face the faith practised in those areas of southern Scotland which subsequently came under Northumbrian domination, for example Melrose where St Cuthbert

The head of the Ruthwell Cross, which now stands in a specially-constructed apse in Ruthwell Parish Church. The top of the monument has apparently been replaced the wrong way round.

received his education after 651, were a fecund amalgam of ancient British and Roman practice.

After Edwin's death a further twist was given to the tale of Northumbrian conversion by the accession to the throne in c. 633 of Aethelfrith's son, Oswald. Like Edwin, he had been converted to the Christian faith by Britons while in exile among them. Oswald's affection for the Columban way was clearly deep-rooted, for about two years after he had secured himself in Northumbria he invited a monk from Iona, named Aidan, to take charge of the Anglian church. As Abbot of Lindisfarne and Bishop of Northumbria Aidan oversaw a remarkable flowering of the church in the region, establishing the tradition of scholarship and Christian-inspired artistic creativity which gave us the spectacular Lindisfarne Gospels, the Ruthwell Cross and Bede's *Ecclesiastical History of the English People*.

The dominance of the British/Celtic church in Northumbria did not last. Oswald's successor, Oswiu (641–670) was also influenced by the Ionan tradition. But after Aidan's death in 651 his successors, Finan and Colman, found themselves deeply embroiled in the controversy between British and Roman practice, which, for the sake of convenience, we may call the Easter dispute. The actual points of disagreement were in fact not of overwhelming importance: even Aidan had accepted that bishops had precedence over abbots when it came to missionary work. What was really at issue was the unity of the Christian church in Britain, and whether a united institution was to be controlled by innovators or conservatives.

In an attempt to settle the matter once and for all, Oswiu summoned a synod to meet at Whitby in 664. Following the death of Dominall Brecc in 642 the power of Dalriada, and with it the influence of the Celtic church, was in decline. Oswiu's sympathies may have lain with the men of Lindisfarne but, as with Edwin before him, political considerations won the day. The king wished to secure his southern frontier in preparation for expansion to the north. In order to do so he came down on the side of the Roman party, whose chief protagonists were the queen, prince Alhfrith and an up-and-coming cleric by the name of Wilfrid. On hearing of the decision, Colman resigned and trekked back to Iona with those monks who supported him.

Though it was many years before the new practices were accepted throughout Scotland, the traditional church there was now unquestionably on the defensive. The majority of the Irish had accepted Roman ways in 630, and about 80 years later Iona and the Pictish church leadership followed suit. This was not the end of

A reconstruction of St John's Cross, Iona. The original eighth-century cross was made in separate pieces and assembled using techniques borrowed from joinery.

the story. In 731 Bede grumbled that the British were still adhering to 'their own wicked practices, rejecting the true Easter of the Roman Church'. And even in the early Middle Ages there were still complaints of Celtic irregularities within the Scottish church. True ecclesiastical uniformity came only when Scotland had been forged into one nation under a single powerful king.

The Synod of Whitby was followed by what appears to have been a bout of blatant ecclesiastical imperialism, for which its perpetrator, Wilfrid, was later rewarded with canonisation. Created Bishop of Northumbria shortly after the Roman theological triumph of 664, he used the campaigns of Oswiu and Ecgfrith against the Celtic north to translate the Whitby decision into action. As far as we can tell, the new bishop encouraged the warriors of Northumbria to drive the British clergy forcibly from newly conquered areas, thereby ensuring that where the writ of the Anglian King ran, there the writ of Wilfrid ran also. By the time of his death in 709 the Bishop of Northumbria's province stretched from Lindisfarne to the Solway Firth, where the Ruthwell and Bewcastle Crosses are believed to have been raised to mark the extent of Wilfrid's rather than Christ's influence.

The employment of the Roman church as a cultural steamroller in the wake of the Northumbrian advance was almost certainly disliked by the native populations whom it sought to crush, and the degree to which the Roman Catholic Church was accepted is uncertain. Bishop Trumwine of Abercorn in Lothian made a pretty hasty exit to the south after the defeat of Northumbrian forces by the Picts in 685. There is evidence to suggest, however, that the see itself did not collapse. It was overbearing Northumbrians who were resented, not their faith. Missionaries from among the Northumbrians who had settled north of the Forth may have played an important part in converting the peoples of southern Pictland.

The extension of the rule of Rome to Iona and Northern Pictland was achieved peacefully. In about 712 the elderly Anglo-Saxon bishop Egbert arrived in Iona from Ireland and managed to persuade the monks there to adopt Catholic ways. The fact that the church in Ireland was at this time at the height of its influence must have aided him in his task. The troubled reign of King Nechtan of Pictland began in about 706. As a convinced Christian, the king must have worried over the British–Roman division in the church almost as much as he did over the problem of holding on to his throne. After about 710, therefore, he hit upon a way of tackling both difficulties at the same time.

The site of Scotland's oldest church? The supremely important archaeological excavations taking place at Whithorn in the summer of 1990.

The plan was not dissimilar to those followed by Edwin and Oswiu in the previous century. Nechtan's court still followed Columban church customs, a practice which did not endear the king to his potentially dangerous neighbours in the south. Therefore, in search of ecclesiastical enlightenment and a possible political rapprochement, he sent a high-level delegation to Northumbria. Its mission was to ask Abbot Ceolfrith of Jarrow to explain exactly why the Picts should move over to the Roman church. As an incidental bonus, Nechtan also requested Ceolfrith to send north:

> architects who knew how to build a stone church, like those used by the Roman Catholics. Nechtan promised that if Ceolfrith did so he would dedicate the building to St Peter, and the Picts and their king would follow the practices of the holy apostolic church of Rome, in so far as that was possible given the physical remoteness of their territory. (Bede)

Bede was at Jarrow when the embassy from the north arrived, so he must have met these alien people whose language few understood. He relates the incident in full, even citing the whole of Ceolfrith's lengthy reply to the Picts' questions. We cannot be certain of the outcome of Nechtan's ploy. He probably kept his side of the bargain with Ceolfrith and abandoned the traditional church customs. In about 717 he ordered all Columban monks in Pictland to return to Iona, though by this time the island community itself had also moved to Rome, and for a while the Picts and the Northumbrians seemed to have lived at peace with each other. Nevertheless, Nechtan's career did not become any easier, and in spite of the accord with the Picts he finally lost his throne to Oengus in 729.

Christianity had taken a long time to reach the whole of the Pictish people, but they took to the new faith with obvious relish. Despite their civil upheavals and the repercussions of the Easter dispute, during the eighth century the church in Pictland inspired a delightful cultural resurgence. Its artists produced the remarkable series of carved stones already mentioned (see chapter 7) and there is evidence of Pictish influence on works of art being fashioned as far away as Iona. Thus, by the time of the first Viking assaults, the people of Scotland shared a common faith and thereby to some extent a common culture.

10

TOWARDS A
NEW NATION

The Norsemen

S T BLATHMAC'S early career in several ways resembled that of St Columba, the holy man for whom he developed an unstinting admiration. Both were distinguished members of the Irish warrior class who renounced the values and traditions of their upbringing, exchanging their weapons for prayer books in order to concentrate on the subtle and enduring delights of the hereafter. Both died on Iona, Columba in 597, Blathmac in 825 – but in the manner of their passing any resemblance between their lives ends abruptly.

After a day of prayer and quiet pastoral duty, the aged Columba breathed his last while lying peacefully in bed. He had had a premonition that he was about to die and he met his end with blessed serenity. When Blathmac awoke to face his last day on earth, he too had a fairly good idea that he would not live to see nightfall. Yet he was neither ill nor infirm. Like Columba, he took comfort from the island community's regular daily routine of prayer. But while standing at the altar celebrating mass he heard a terrible noise outside. The story is taken up by Strabo, an Ionan monk who later wrote a long poem describing the life and death of his hero:

> Then a gang of violent barbarians burst into the building through its open doors. Cursing and swearing, they slaughtered all the monks attending the service. This done, they turned upon the unarmed Blathmac and demanded that he tell them the whereabouts of the shrine of St Columba, with its hoard of precious metal.

Blathmac, who had known of the presence of a band of Viking marauders in the vicinity and may even have been approached by them beforehand with some sort of commercial deal, refused even under torture to reveal where the treasure was hidden. He almost certainly wished for a martyr's death, and when their patience ran out the Vikings duly obliged by tearing him limb from limb.

The fate meted out by the Vikings to Blathmac and his fellow monks was in no way unusual. The prolonged period of Norse assault to which the Scottish kingdoms were subjected from the late eighth century onwards was of almost unbelievable ferocity and cruelty. It shook the Celtic Christian civilisation of the Dark Ages to its very core and occasioned a fundamental reconstruction of the political map of the country. It also turned out to be the furnace in which a new unity was forged.

In 800, authority in the region above Hadrian's Wall was principally divided between the Scots of Dalriada, the Picts, the surviving British kingdom of Strathclyde and the Northumbrians of the south-east. Two centuries later only the Scots remained in power, and no longer merely as masters of a small coastal principality. Though they had to recognise Norse supremacy over large tracts of the north and west, by 1018 the rule of the Scottish kings of Alba (as their kingdom was at first known) extended from the Great Glen to an indeterminate frontier region along the Solway-Tweed line. The new power in the north was coming to be called by a different name, too: Scotland.

There have been several attempts in recent years to soften the popular image of the Vikings as pathological killers who delighted in destruction, cruelty and murder. It is true that since history was written by the monks, and vulnerable seaside monasteries made soft targets for shiploads of booty-seekers, tales of Viking excesses lost nothing in the telling. But even allowing for gross exaggeration, the ghastly deeds of wanton inhumanity perpetrated by the attackers were far in excess of anything practised by native warriors. The Celtic punishment of drowning, for example, was mildness itself compared with the horrifying Viking custom of 'blood-eagling':

Earl Einar cut a bloody eagle into his enemy's back – placing his sword on the victim's spine, he hacked all the ribs away from the backbone, down as far as the loins. Einar then pulled out the lungs and offered them to Odin as a gesture of thanks for his victory.

Those who despoiled monasteries, burned farms and slaughtered untold thousands were probably the most desperate members of a particularly uncouth society. As in Europe at the time of the crusades, the least desirable members of the community and those who had little to lose were prepared to set off into the unknown in search of glory and plunder. In time the Viking storm troops were followed by groups of Scandinavian settlers. Efforts to clean up the Viking image have tended to blur the distinction between the first warbands and later, more pacific visitors.

The earliest Scandinavian raiders came from western Norway. In the ninth century, the pattern of assault was complicated by the appearance of Danish warriors, who soon came into conflict with the original marauders. In 850, for example, there was fighting in the Western Isles when the Danes tried to loosen their rivals' hold over the region. Later still, counter-raids were launched against Scandinavia from Britain. By this time Norse operations were no longer small-scale private enterprise ventures, but involved considerable fleets of vessels assembled at royal command.

Though large migrations of peoples were a common enough historical phenomena, we are still not sure precisely why they took place. Single explanations, such as overpopulation or climate change, are clearly inadequate. They can just as easily lead to adjustments within a nation as to expansion. Furthermore, they hardly explain the extent of the outward drive: it was no more necessary for the Mongols of central Asia to carve out the largest land empire in world history to solve the internal problems of Mongolia, for example, than it was for the Vikings to deal with land shortage in Scandinavia by moving as far afield as Britain, Ireland, France and Russia. If the peoples of the north were simply looking for *lebensraum*, then there was a certain overkill in the measures they adopted. In short, though the nations of Scandinavia may have been destabilised by a rising population towards the end of the first millennium AD, the precise nature of their response to the situation was determined by a complex interaction of social and cultural factors which has yet to be understood. Fortunately, from a Scottish point of view it is not so much the reasons for Norse expansion which concern us here as the consequences.

The success of the initial Viking attacks is not hard to understand. Firstly, the Norsemen had the element of surprise. For the previous 300 years, the Scottish kingdoms had engaged in sporadic land warfare. As the positing of monasteries in remote island or coastal sites illustrates, seaborne assault was wholly unexpected.

A partly reconstructed Viking house at Whithorn, Dumfries and Galloway.

The Viking longboat, the culmination of centuries of technological development, was the perfect vehicle with which to launch sudden long-range raids. The vessels' shallow draught allowed them to be easily piloted right up to the shore or deep inland along lochs or rivers. Their flexible, keeled construction gave the craft remarkable seaworthiness, and the combination of oar, rudder and sail enabled them to make swift headway in all but the most violent weather conditions.

Finally, the Odin-worshipping warriors from the north were steeped in an unremitting battle culture which prized military success, whether achieved by force of arms or guile, above all else. They sought no greater glory than to die knowing that their name would be recalled in saga for generations to come, as 'the skull cleaver', the 'widow maker' or, more prosaically, simply as 'the lean', 'flatnose', 'the red' or 'fine hair'. Mercy and pity found no place in the hearts of men driven by a fierce thirst for bloody fame and the spoils of the campaign. Thus in the bitter northern culture clash of the ninth century, the more gentle Christian civilisation of Picts, Scots, Angles and Britons started at a considerable disadvantage, and it was many years before they managed to halt the onslaught which threatened to overwhelm them.

The first recorded Viking raid was made on Lindisfarne in 793. Major attacks followed the next year. Skye was the target in 795, Ireland the next year and mainland Scotland in 798. Starting in 802, Iona was ravaged time and again, and after the 806 assault many of the monks fled to Kells in Ireland. Yet, owing to the self-sacrifice of men such as Blathmac, the community miraculously survived to become a major Christian centre for both Celts and Norse in calmer times. The first Norse settlements were made in the second quarter of the ninth century; within 25 years they had become permanent. The occupied areas were largely in the north and west, above the Great Glen: the Orkney and Shetland isles, Caithness, Sutherland, the western seaboard (including Kintyre and parts of Galloway) and the Hebrides as far south as Islay. Dalriada was finally cut off from Ireland. When in the second part of the ninth century the Scandinavians successfully colonised large areas of Northumbria, the Celts of Scotland found themselves locked within a beleaguered outpost of Chistian civilisation.

The fate of those living in areas which fell to the Vikings is uncertain. It seems that the native inhabitants of the Orkneys and Shetlands either fled south or were killed. On the other hand, in the Hebrides and on the mainland there was no such total replacement of the existing population, though they were often forced into slavery. In the course of time the conquerors and the vanquished interbred, and by the eleventh century we find the Gaelic language re-emerging as the common tongue on some of the Western Isles, suggesting that the superimposed Viking culture may have been comparatively shallow-rooted. In the regions where the Norsemen settled, Scandinavian place names are plentiful, accounting for virtually all such names in the Northern Isles. *Inse Orc* became *Orkneyjar* (from which we derive Orkney), for example. Other clues to the whereabouts of Viking settlement are afforded by words incorporating the suffixes -*nish* (meaning promontory, as in Vaternish on Skye), -*val* (meaning mountain, as in the Shetland island of Yell), -*ay* (meaning island, as in Islay), and incorporating words such as *wick* (meaning a bay, as in Lerwick on Shetland) or *dale* (meaning a valley, as in Helmsdale in Sutherland).

The nature of the Norse settlements really lies beyond the scope of this book, although it is worth noting that they were not fundamentally different from those they replaced. There were new styles of ornament and building, but the Scandinavian settlers were farmers, fishermen, metalworkers and traders just as those they replaced had been. They worked the same land as their predecessors and in some cases must have taken over their dwellings. The extent to which Christianity survived in Viking areas is uncertain – it may have been tolerated among the servile classes, but it was several centuries before all the new arrivals had been converted to the faith of the rest of Britain. The status of women in Viking society was quite high, and it may not have been improved by the advent of Christianity.

By the middle of the ninth century, the Norsemen (known as *Lochlannaich* to the indigenous population) had become a permanent feature of the Scottish political scene. No longer regarded simply as uncivilised barbarians whose hit-and-run raids terrorised all those living within easy reach of the sea, they had begun to have a crucial impact on the relations between the four major power blocs. In fact, there is a real possibility that Kenneth mac Alpin, whom popular tradition venerates as the first King of Scots, owed much of his celebrated success to the influence and perhaps even the assistance of the Vikings.

The Triumph of the Scots

We will probably never know precisely how Kenneth mac Alpin became king of a united Scottish and Pictish kingdom in the middle of the ninth century. After the death of King Oengus I of Picts in 761, the sources become particularly confusing. Those from Iona stop in about 740, and the usually reliable supply of Northumbrian information dries up in the ninth century, when the Vikings took over north-east England. There are king lists for the period, but they are difficult to interpret: from the later part of the reign of King Constantine (c. 789–c. 820) onwards, for example, we have two separate lists for Dalriada and also two for Pictland. The division between Pict and Scot becomes blurred as a number of figures of Scottish descent managed to establish themselves as kings of both Dalriada and Pictland. This may well detract from the originality of Kenneth mac Alpin's position. What it does not call into question, however, is his achievement in winning the combined overlordship for a hitherto little-known Scottish family.

As mentioned in chapter 7, when Oengus I died the Pictish king was almost certainly in control of Dalriada. But it was also noted that Oengus may well have been part Scot (his name is Gaelic), so his forays to the west could be interpreted as attempts to win a throne to which he felt he had a reasonable claim. He was succeeded by his brother Bridei, then by King Kenneth who in 768 was defeated by Aed Find of Dalriada (c. 758–c. 778) in Fortriu.

The site of this battle is important. Fortriu was an eastern kingdom based in the region of Perth, and the presence there of the Scots in the eighth century suggests that at this early stage Dalriada was already beginning the drive to the east normally associated with its victory over the Picts in the next century. Aed was clearly more than a mere warrior, for later kings of Alba were to reissue the celebrated 'Laws' which he supposedly promulgated.

The next figure of consequence is King Constantine, son of a Pictish princess and Fergus of the *Cenel Gabrain* (Aed's successor in Dalriada). Constantine is credited with a very long reign as King of Pictland. He was also King of Dalriada from about 811 after overcoming local kings there. The choice of the name of the first Christian Roman emperor for a member of a remote northern royal family is an illuminating insight into the extent to which Christianity and classical learning had entered Pictish-Dalriadic society by this time. It may also tell us something of the political pretensions of those who christened the child.

The problem of working out who was king of where, and to which kingdom their primary allegiance lay, is exemplified by the fact that Constantine won the Pictish throne by defeating one Conall, son of Tadg, in what has been cited as a Pictish civil war. Yet Conall went on to become king of Dalriada until killed and

The carvings and inscriptions which cover the Ruthwell Cross (Dumfries and Galloway) were intended as a permanent lesson in early Roman Catholic scripture. The cross may have been erected in Dumfries to mark the furthest limit of Northumbrian ecclesiastical influence in the late seventh century.

A detail from the Ruthwell Cross, one of Britain's finest Dark-Age monuments, portraying Mary Magdalene washing the feet of Christ.

replaced on the throne by another Conall (son of Aedan) in 807!

Enough of this confusing genealogical gallimaufry. From the layman's point of view, the important features of Constantine's reign were his Scottish ancestry, his simultaneous reign in Dalriada and Pictland, and his building of a church at Dunkeld in Fortriu, which was later to become a major Alban ecclesiastical centre. The move suggests an eastward drift of the Celtic church, away from the vulnerable west coast, mirrored in a similar shift in Dalriadic political power. What appears to be happening, therefore, is that the Scots are tightening their grip on Pictland while at the same time establishing a new headquarters in the east, away from their traditional power base in Dalriada which Norse attacks were making increasingly untenable.

Constantine was succeeded as King of Dalriada and Pictland by his brother Oengus II (c. 820–c. 834). During his reign the eastward movement of the church away from Iona was further advanced by the re-establishment of a major church at St Andrews. The obscure kings Drest and Talorgen then ruled in Pictland until replaced in 837 by Oengus's son Eoganan, who also seized control of Dalriada, thereby restoring the joint rule of his predecessors. Now we come to the crucial battle of 839, fought somewhere in Fortriu. In this momentous clash between a Christian force and the *Lochlannaich*, Eoganan and many members of both the Pictish and Dalriadic royal families were slain.

Of the man who took advantage of the power vacuum left by the slaughter of 839 we know almost nothing. Alpin's ancestors were probably a lesser branch of the ruling clique of the *Cenel Gabrain*, and there is no concrete evidence that he was regarded as King of Dalriada before 839. A prestigious ancestry was probably invented for him later in order to lend weight to his son's claim to the throne of Alba. Alpin may have had a Pictish or even a Norse wife, for the surprising speed with which his fortunes rose after the death of Eoganan may be explained by the fact that Alpin and his son Kenneth were in league with the barbarians. If this was the case, then Alpin was an aristocratic western warlord, isolated from the Pictish-Dalriadic power base in Fortriu, who cleverly manipulated the dangerous political situation to his own advantage by temporarily siding with the Vikings to clear his path to the throne of Dalriada. He then spent two years fighting to extend his authority, dying in about 841 in Galloway.

Kenneth mac Alpin continued where his father had left off, moving into Fortriu two years later. He had little choice. As previous monarchs had realised, Dalriada was now a hard-pressed frontier region where no league with the

Scandinavians could be expected to hold for long. Kenneth's position as ruler of Dalriada and Pictland was not a new one: as we have seen, Constantine, Oengus II and Eoganan (briefly) had all held it before him. What was new was that Kenneth was first and foremost a Scot: he did not contemplate a merger of the two kingdoms, but a total conquest of Pictland.

Conflicting Pictish king lists speak of a number of native monarchs succeeding Eoganan (or Uuen as he is known in Pictish), until the line died out around 849. Clearly Kenneth's seizure of power did not go unchallenged. Later stories speak of his using treachery to overcome his opponents, the sort of Machiavellian tactic which one might expect from a man who had previouly stooped to employing the pagans to remove his opponents. One fable tells how Kenneth invited the Pictish aristocracy to a great feast, then murdered them when they were tipsy. Another relates how he called them to some sort of council attended by his own followers with weapons hidden beneath their robes. At a prearranged signal in the middle of the proceedings, the Scots produced their swords and massacred their Pictish rivals. Though both these tales are undoubtedly apocryphal, they are an indication that the Kingdom of Alba was not created peacefully. They also suggest that, when it came to dirty tricks, the stock of Alpin had learned a thing or two from their erstwhile Norse allies.

From this time forward a distinct Pictish culture rapidly disappears. The agricultural land of eastern Scotland was superior to that of the west, and Kenneth's political success may well have been followed by a migration of Scots to former Pictish territory. The Pictish language died out and Scots laws (or rather those codified by Aed) were later imposed upon Pict and Scot alike. In 848, part of the remains of St Columba were transferred from Iona to Dunkeld, emphasising the totality of the Scots' conquest. The importance of the ancient religious centre was never entirely forgotten, however, and it was felt to be a suitable resting place for the remains of many future kings of Alba.

The swift and complete eclipse of the Picts is one of the mysteries of Scottish history. The whole population can hardly have been wiped out. It is more likely that the majority, deprived of their leaders and subjected to an unremitting Scottish overlordship, in time simply merged with the conquerors. Moreover, once Kenneth had established himself, the Christian kingdom of Alba had more important things to think about than preserving the distinctions between Pict and Scot. At the time of Kenneth's death in c. 858, his kingdom was hard pressed on all sides by the hostile Norse. Just as their activity had enabled Alpin and his son to set up their new kingdom, so their continued presence served to give it a real sense of identity.

Ancient to Modern

The achievement of Kenneth mac Alpin became clear only long after his death. To contemporaries the merger of the Picts with the Scots might have appeared merely as a desperate attempt to pool resources in the face of the ever more pressing danger from the Vikings, and on several future occasions it appeared as if Alba might disappear beneath the Scancinavian wave. At other times the English seemed the greater threat, as when King Athelstan roundly defeated all the peoples of the north at the Battle of Brunanburgh in 937.

Yet Kenneth's Alba proved remarkably resilient. It was able not only to resist assaults upon its territory but also to expand. Strathclyde was annexed in 900. A little over a century later Kenneth mac Alpin's great-great-great grandson, Malcolm II, finally secured Lothian for the Scottish crown. The extension of Scottish authority northwards was more difficult, but at the Treaty of Perth in 1266 the kingdom finally recovered from Norway all that remained of the Scandinavian empire established more than 400 years previously.

There are few, if any, events in the past which can without qualification be labelled turning points. The accession of Kenneth mac Alpin is no exception, for there had been other kings who ruled simultaneously over both Picts and Scots. Yet, with his seizure of power, Scottish history takes on a sharper focus. No longer is the scene lit by four separate spotlights of roughly equal brightness, but by one major beam and a number of lesser shafts. And in time the greater eclipses the lesser, spreading outwards to cover the whole country. When this happens we are no longer dealing with the ancient Scotland of myth and monument, but with a new and altogether different country.

A brief chronology of ancient Scotland

(NB All dates for prehistoric times are little better than estimates)

Date

BC

	Palaeolithic period c. 1,000,000 BC to c. 15,000 BC
c. 40000	*Homo sapiens sapiens* appears in Europe
c. 15000	Last Ice Age ending

	Mesolithic period c. 15,000 BC to c. 4500 BC
c. 7000	Man first appears in Scotland
c. 5500	Britain becomes an island

	Neolithic period c. 4500 BC to c. 2000 BC
c. 3000	Earliest chambered tombs built
c. 2500	First stone circles erected
c. 2650	Beginning of the Beaker period
c. 2600	First copper objects

	Bronze Age c. 2000 BC to c. 700 BC
c. 2000	Bronze working
	Chambered communal tombs go out of fashion
	Cist burials common

c. 1100	Marked deterioration in the climate begins
	Burial sites no longer constructed
c. 1000	Defensive settlements become common

	Iron Age/Roman period c. 700 BC to c. 400 AD
c. 600	Celts appear in Scotland; iron working
55	Julius Caesar's first expedition to Britain

AD

43	Emperor Claudius invades Britain
81–84	Agricola's expedition into Caledonia
84	Battle of Mons Graupius
85	Romans begin to abandon positions in Scotland
122	Work begins on Hadrian's Wall
143	Work begins on the Antonine Wall

c. 155–
  c. 200   Romans retreat from Scotland
c. 208   Severus invades Scotland
  211   Romans withdraw to Hadrian's
         Wall
c. 250   First Christians in Scotland
  297   Earliest mention of Picts
c. 306–
  c. 310   Emperor Constantine restores
         Roman position in northern
         Britain
  342   Fresh assaults on Roman Britain
  367   'Barbarian Conspiracy': massive
         attack on Britannia
  370   Theodosius restores Roman
         position in the north
c. 380   Final withdrawal of Roman forces
         from Scotland
c. 400   Ninian arrives in Galloway

Dark Ages c. 400 AD to c. 1000 AD

c. 400   Angles begin to settle in Deira
c. 407   Last Roman troops leave Britain
c. 497   Fergus Mor arrives in western
         Scotland from Dal Riata
c. 500   'The Age of Arthur'
c. 520–
  c. 612   St Kentigern
521–
  597   St Columba
c. 547   Foundation of Bernicia
c. 558   Death of Gabran, King of Dalriada
  563   Columba arrives in Scotland
c. 570–
  c. 590   Urien king of Rheged
574–
  608   Aedan king of Dalriada
  584   Death of Bridei, son of Maelcon,
         King of Picts
c. 593–
  c. 617   Aethelfrith king of Bernicia

c. 600   Warriors of Gododdin and other
         British kingdoms defeated by
         Angles at Catterick
c. 603   Battle of Degsastan: Aedan of
         Dalriada defeated by Bernicians
c. 612   Bernicia and Deira first united
         into Kingdom of Northumbria
  617   Martyrdom of St Donan
c. 617–
  c. 633   Edwin king of Northumbria
  627   Edwin baptised into Roman
         church by Paulinus
c. 630–
  c. 643   Domnall Brecc king of Dalriada
c. 633–
  c. 643   Oswald king of Northumbria
  638   Edinburgh besieged, perhaps by
         Northumbrians
c. 650   Class I Pictish stones first produced
  651   Death of Aidan, Bishop of
         Lindisfarne
  655   Oswiu King of a united
         Northumbria
  658   Oswiu of Northumbria invades
         southern Pictland
  664   Synod of Whitby
  672   Unsuccessful revolt of southern
         Picts against Northumbrians
672–
  693   Bridei, son of Bili, king of Picts
  673   Monastery founded at Applecross
         by St Maelrubbha
c. 680   Northumbrian conquest of
         Rheged complete
  681   Northumbrian bishopric founded
         at Abercorn
  685   Northumbrians driven from
         Pictland
  697   'Law of the Innocents'
         promulgated

c. 700	Class II Pictish stones first produced	806	Monks from Iona move to Kells
c. 706–		c. 811	Constantine king of Dalriada
724	Nechtan king of Picts	c. 820–	
709	Death of St Wilfrid, Bishop of Northumbria	c. 834	Oengus II king of Picts and Scots
711	Picts defeated by Northumbrians at Battle of Manaw	825	Martyrdom of St Blathmac at Iona by Vikings
712	Iona accepts Roman Catholic practices	837–839	Eoganan king of Picts and Scots
c. 717	Iona's monks expelled from Pictland	839	Scottish and Pictish forces defeated by Vikings in Fortriu Alpin king of Dalriada
729–		841	Kenneth mac Alpin king of Dalriada
761	Oengus I King of Picts		
731	Northumbrian bishop in Whithorn	c. 843	Kenneth mac Alpin begins conquest of Pictland
733	Oengus invades Dalriada	848	Part of the remains of St Columba moved from Iona to Dunkeld
756	Oengus of Picts and Eadberht of Northumbria defeated at Dumbarton in Strathclyde	c. 849	Ruling line of Pictish kings dies out
c. 758–		c. 850	Norse settlements in north and west acquiring permanence
c. 778	Aed king of Dalriada		
c. 789–		c. 858	Death of Kenneth mac Alpin, King of Alba
c. 820	Constantine king of Picts		
793	Viking attack on Lindisfarne	866	Danish conquest of Northumbria begins
795	Viking raids on Skye		
802	Iona ravaged by Vikings	900	Alba annexes Strathclyde
803	Last Northumbrian bishop leaves Whithorn	1018	Battle of Carham: Lothian ceded to Scottish crown

Bibliography

Alcock, L., *Arthur's Britain: History and Archaeology, 367–634*, London, 1971

Anderson, A. O., *Early Sources of Scottish History AD 500 to 1286*, 2 vols., Edinburgh, 1922.

..... and M. O., (eds), *Adomnan's Life of Columba*, Edinburgh, 1961.

Anderson, M. O., *Kings and Kingship in Early Scotland*, Edinburgh, 1973.

....., *Scottish Annals from English Chroniclers*, Edinburgh, 1968.

Bannerman, J., *Studies in the History of Dalriada*, Edinburgh, 1974.

Bede, *A History of the English Church and People*, translated by L. Sherley Price, London, 1955.

Breeze, D. J., *The Northern Frontiers of Roman Britain*, London, 1982.

Burl, A., *Prehistoric Stone Circles*, Aylesbury, 1988.

Chadwick, N., *The Celts*, London, 1971.

....., *The British Heroic Age*, Cardiff, 1976.

Colgrave, B., (ed.), *Two Lives of St Cuthbert*, reprinted New York, 1969.

Crawford, B., *Scandinavian Scotland*, Leicester, 1987.

Cunliffe, B., *Iron Age Communities in Britain*, London, 1974.

Darvill, T., *Prehistoric Britain*, London, 1987.

Delaney, F., *The Celts*, London, 1986.

Dickinson, W. C. (Revised by A. A. M. Duncan), *Scotland, From Earliest Times to 1603*, Oxford, 1977.

Dodgshon, R. A., *Land and Society in Early Scotland*, Oxford, 1982.

Donaldson, G., *The Faith of the Scots*, London, 1990.

....., *Scottish Historical Documents*, Edinburgh, 1974.

....., and Morpeth, R. S., *Who's Who in Scottish History*, Edinburgh, 1973.

Dunbar, A. H., *Scottish Kings*, Edinburgh, 2nd edn, 1906.

Duncan, A. A. M., *Scotland: The Making of the Kingdom*, reprinted Edinburgh, 1989.

Dyer, J., *Ancient Britain*, London, 1990.

Exploring Scotland's Heritage, Royal Commission on the Ancient and Historical Monuments of Scotland, 8 vols, various authors, H.M.S.O., 1985–7.

Farrell, R. T., (ed.), *The Vikings*, London, 1982.

Feacham, R. W., *Guide to Prehistoric Scotland*, London, 1977.

Forde-Johnston, J., *Hadrian's Wall*, London, 1978.

Frere, S., *Britannia: A History of Roman Britain*, London, 2nd edn, 1967.

Handbook of British Chronology, Royal Historical Society, 2nd edn, London, 1961.

Henderson, I., *The Picts*, London, 1967.

Hughes, K., *Celtic Britain in the Early Middle Ages: Studies in Scottish and Welsh Sources*, (ed. Dumville, D.), London, 1980.

Jackson, K. H., *The Gododdin, The Oldest Scottish Poem*, Edinburgh, 1968.

Johnson, S., *English Heritage: Hadrian's Wall*, London, 1989.

Laing, L., *Ancient Scotland*, Newton Abbott, 1976.

....., *Britain Before the Conquest*, London, 1987.

..... and J., *A Guide to the Dark Age Remains in Britain*, London, 1979.

MacSween, A., and Sharp, M., *Prehistoric Scotland*, London, 1989.

Mann, J. C., *The Northern Frontier in Britain from Hadrian to Honorius: Literary and Epigraphic Sources*, Oxford, 1969.

Menzies, G., (ed.) *Who Are the Scots?*, Edinburgh, 1971.

New History of Scotland, 8 vols, London, 1981.

Piggott, S., *Ancient Europe*, Edinburgh, 1965.

....., (ed.), *The Prehistoric Peoples of Scotland*, Edinburgh, 1962.

....., *Scotland before History*, Edinburgh, 1958.

Renfrew, C., (ed.), *British Prehistory*, London, 1974.

Reynolds, P. J., *Iron Age Farm*, London, 1979.

Richmond, I. A., (ed.), *Roman and Native in North Britain*, Oxford, 1958.

Ritchie, G. and A., *Scotland: Archaeology and Early History*, London, 1981.

Ritchie, J. N. G., *Brochs of Scotland*, Aylesbury, 1988.

Rivet, A. L. F., (ed.), *The Iron Age in Northern Britain*, Edinburgh, 1967.

Robertson, A. S., *The Antonine Wall*, Glasgow, 3rd edn, 1979.

Ross, A., *The Pagan Celts*, London, 1986.

Ross, S., *Monarchs of Scotland*, Moffat, 1990.

....., *Scottish Castles*, Moffat, 1990.

Salway, P., *Roman Britain*, Oxford, 1981.

Sawyer, P. H., *Kings and Vikings: Scandinavia and Europe AD 700–1100*, London, 1982.

Skene, W. F., (ed.), *Chronicles of the Picts, Chronicles of the Scots and Other Early Memorials of Scottish History*, Edinburgh, 1867.

Simpson, D. D. A., *Economy and Settlement in Neolithic and Early Bronze Age Britain and Europe*, Oxford, 1971.

Smyth, A. P., *Warlords and Holy Men, Scotland AD 80–1000*, Edinburgh, 1989.

....., *Scandinavian Kings in the British Isles, 850–80*, Oxford, 1977.

....., *Scandinavian York and Dublin*, 2 vols, Dublin and New Jersey, 1980.

Stenton, F., *Anglo-Saxon England*, Oxford, 2nd. edn, 1947.

Tacitus, *The Agricola and the Germania*, translated by H. Mattingly, revised by S. A. Handford, London, 1970.

Thomas, C., *Celtic Britain*, London, 1986.

....., *Christianity in Roman Britain to AD 500*, London, 1981.

....., *Early Christian Archaeology of North Britain*, London and Glasgow, 1971.

Wacher, J., *Roman Britain*, London, 1978.

Wainwright, F. T., (ed.), *The Problem of the Picts*, Edinburgh, 1955.

Whitlock, D., with Douglas, D. C. and Tucker, S. I., *Anglo-Saxon Chronicle*, London, 1961.

Wood, M., *Saga-Book of the Viking Society*, London, 1980.

Index